Civil Rights, The White House, and the Justice Department 1945–1968

A 20 volume Series of Key Documents in Facsimile

Edited with Introductions by
Michal R. Belknap
Professor of Law
California Western School of Law

A Garland Series

CONTENTS OF THE SERIES

1. Attitudes, Goals, and Priorities
2. Presidential Committees and White House Conferences
3. Integration of the Armed Forces
4. Employment of Blacks by the Federal Government
5. Equal Employment Opportunity
6. Combatting Housing Discrimination
7. Desegregation of Public Education
8. Desegregation of Public Transportation, Facilities, and Programs
9. The Drive to Desegregate Places of Public Accommodation
10. Racial Violence and Law Enforcement in the South
11. Urban Race Riots
12. Securing the Enactment of Civil Rights Legislation: 1946–1960
13. Securing the Enactment of Civil Rights Legislation: Civil Rights Act of 1964
14. Securing the Enactment of Civil Rights Legislation: 1965–1968
15. Voting Rights
16. Justice Department Civil Rights Policies Prior to 1960: Crucial Documents from the Files of Arthur Brann Caldwell
17. Administrative History of the Civil Rights Division of the Department of Justice During the Johnson Administration (2 volumes)
18. Justice Department Briefs in Crucial Civil Rights Cases: 1948–1968 (2 volumes)

VOLUME 2

Presidential Committees and White House Conferences

Introduction by
Michal R. Belknap

Garland Publishing, Inc.
New York & London 1991

The editor and publisher are grateful to the Harry S. Truman, Dwight D. Eisenhower, John Fitzgerald Kennedy, and Lyndon Baines Johnson Libraries, and to the University of Arkansas for permission to reproduce the documents included in this series.

Library of Congress Cataloging-in-Publication Data

Presidential committees and White House Conferences.
p. cm. — (Civil rights, the White House, and the Justice Department, 1945–1968 ; v. 2)
ISBN 0-8240-3368-X (alk. paper)
1. Afro-Americans—Civil rights—History—20th century—Sources. 2. Civil rights movements—United States—History—20th century—Sources. 3. United States. President's Committee on Civil Rights—History—Sources. 4 White House Conference "To Fulfill These Rights" (1966 : Washington, D.C.)—History—Sources. I. Series.
E185.61.P756 1991
353.0081'1—dc20 91-3628

Design by Marisel Tavárez

INTRODUCTION

This volume examines two important efforts to involve private citizens in the formulation of federal civil rights policy. One of these occurred at the beginning of the era covered by *Civil Rights, the White House, and the Justice Department, 1945–1968*. The other came near the end of that era, after Supreme Court decisions, such as *Brown* v. *Board of Education,* 347 U.S. 483 (1954), and the enactment of legislation, such as the Civil Rights Act of 1964 and the Voting Rights Act of 1965, had substantially transformed the legal parameters of American race relations. A comparison of the agendas and recommendations of the President's Committee on Civil Rights, which Harry Truman created by executive proclamation in December 1946, and the White House Conference on Civil Rights, which Lyndon Johnson convened in June 1966, provides useful insights into what was accomplished during the two decades after World War II and what remained to be done even after the climax of the Second Reconstruction.

In 1946 African-Americans still occupied a clearly subordinate position in the campaign to improve their own position in American society. The President's Committee on Civil Rights had a white chairman, General Electric President Charles E. Wilson, and only two of its members, attorney Sadie T. M. Alexander and Dr. Channing Tobias, were black. It was charged with studying the whole spectrum of civil rights, and the report that it published made thirty-four quite varied recommendations, ranging from the reorganization of the Civil Rights Section of the Department of Justice, through the enactment of legislation making lynching a federal crime, to the granting of citizenship to the people of Guam and American Samoa. This report was published under the title *To Secure These Rights* (New York, 1947), and for that reason it is not included in this volume. Many significant documents related to the work of the committee are, however.

So are some of the important documents bearing on the work of the 1966 White House Conference. These depict a meeting dominated by the black leadership of major civil rights organizations. They also disclose that, unlike Truman's committee, Johnson's White House Conference focused its attention on four critical areas of living and citizenship: education, housing, the administration of justice, and security and welfare. By the time its participants assembled, many of the objectives of the President's Committee had been achieved. Four administrations had worked to eradicate segregation from the nation's capital. The poll tax had been outlawed and federal legislation enacted prohibiting voting discrimination. The courts had prohibited the segregation of public schools, and Congress had banned discrimination in private employment. Yet, while much of what the President's Committee recommended had been accomplished, a good deal had not been. Like their predecessors, the participants in the White House Conference urged federal action against racist violence and housing discrimination. They also emphasized something that had been less obvious to civil rights advocates two decades earlier: the economic dimension of the plight of African-Americans. By the time

Johnson left the White House in 1969, Congress would have legislated against housing segregation and racially motivated violence and intimidation. Even two decades later, however, some of the problems identified by the White House Conference on Civil Rights, and even the President's Committee on Civil Rights, would remain unsolved.

I would like to express my sincere appreciation to my research assistants: Richard Nover, Erin Gilland-Roby, Jane Ritter, Alicia Borrego, Michael B. Horrow, and Avigal Hoffman. Their hard work and dedication made the assembling of this collection possible.

I would also like to thank California Western School of Law for its financial support of this project.

Michal R. Belknap

CROSS REFERENCE GUIDE

Several other volumes in this series contain documents dealing with the President's Committee on Civil Rights or the White House Conference on Civil Rights. Those documents are listed below. The number before the colon in each entry is the volume number. The numbers after the colon identify documents within that volume. To locate the page number of one of these documents, consult the table of contents for the volume in which it appears.

1: 41

3: 6

5: 52

10: 17

CONTENTS

President's Committee on Civil Rights (Truman Administration)

President's Committee on Civil Rights (Truman Administration)

current law-enforcement measures and the authority and means possessed by Federal, State, and local governments may be strengthened and improved to safeguard the civil rights of the people.

3. All executive departments and agencies of the Federal Government are authorized and directed to cooperate with the Committee in its work, and to furnish the Committee such information or the services of such persons as the Committee may require in the performance of its duties.

4. When requested by the Committee to do so, persons employed in any of the executive departments and agencies of the Federal Government shall testify before the Committee and shall make available for the use of the Committee such documents and other information as the Committee may require.

5. On or before , the Committee shall make a report of its studies to the President in writing, and shall in particular make recommendations with respect to the adoption or establishment, by legislation or otherwise, of more adequate and effective means and procedures for the protection of the civil rights of the people of the United States.

6. Upon rendition of its report to the President, the Committee shall cease to exist, unless otherwise determined by further Executive order.

THE WHITE HOUSE,

October , 1946.

PRESIDENT'S COMMITTEE ON CIVIL RIGHTS.

Minutes of the Meeting Held on January 15, 1947.

- - - - -

The first meeting of the President's Committee on Civil Rights was held at the White House on January 15, 1947. A general discussion took place as to the purposes and aims of the Committee with a view toward getting some form of organization and some plan of procedure for the future work of the Committee.

The Chairman suggested that the following sub-committees be set up:

1. Group to consider and determine if existing legislation is adequate and if found to be inadequate to suggest changes in existing law or any proposed new legislation.

2. Group to consider the broader aspects of the problem including social, economic, and educational programs that should be recommended and adopted. This group should consider the effective utilization of existing organizations and mass media.

3. Group to consider any other related aspects of the Civil Rights question. For example, anti-racial and religious organizations, discrimination, registration statutes and the general problem of anonymity of groups operating in derogation of minority and civil rights.

The Chairman suggested that if three such groups would study the problem, they would pretty well cover the field that is embraced in the franchise the Committee received from the President. A discussion followed as to the advisability of setting up such sub-committees and then Mr. Carey moved as follows: "I move that the recommendation of the Chairman, that three sub-committees be designated, be accepted". The motion was seconded, voted upon, and passed unanimously.

The Chairman was asked to give the members some idea as to how much the Committee would have to spend, either in dollars or in man power. He said that to the best of his knowledge, there would be no limitation put on it; that if it ran into an extraordinary large figure, he would go to the President or somebody else to find out if what the Committee was spending was within the figure that was contemplated. From anything he knew, however, he thought there would be no question about it as he was assured that a pretty substantial organization was contemplated.

Mr. Carey moved: "I would like to make the motion that the

Committee invite national organizations, economic, religious, professional, civic, educational, and cultural, and other organizations, to forward to the Committee a summary report of their activities in the broad field over which this Committee operates." A lengthy discussion followed as to whether the letter calling upon the organizations for their assistance would go to just the "right" organizations or also to bigoted groups. It was decided that it would be a mistake not to write to the bigoted groups and try to get their views and cooperation to enable the Committee to have a complete picture of the whole situation. It was also decided that all groups should be given a chance to submit their views. Mr. Carey said the motion in no way limited the list to the "angels" or the "adversaries", nor was it predicated on the necessity for a hearing. It was that the Committee proceed to announce the desire for this information from these organizations; that a broad press release should be issued first, making it clear that the Committee wanted to accept and seriously consider all groups; that a general invitation should be issued and then specific organizations invited as a second step. The motion was seconded, vote taken, and passed unanimously.

Mrs. Alexander made the following motion: "That this Committee issue a press release inviting organizations concerned with civil rights to report their activities and express their views in writing." Dr. Graham seconded the motion, the vote was taken, and the motion passed unanimously. Mr. Luckman wrote the following release and it was voted that it be submitted to the Press:

> "The President's Committee on Civil Rights can only accomplish the objectives outlined in the President's directive if it truly represents the wishes of the people of this country", stated Mr. Charles E. Wilson, Chairman of the Committee. "No group is capable of interpreting the rights of a free people without adequate expression from all who constitute our democracy", he added. To that end, the Committee earnestly requests that all individuals and groups having a concern with civil rights address to the Committee in Washington, D.C., written communications indicating their activities and views.

A motion was made by Bishop Sherrill that an Executive Committee be appointed to get the preliminary work done and make suggestions to the entire group. This should consist of three members; the Chairman and two appointed as Vice Chairman. The appointment of this committee should be left to the Chairman. Motion was seconded, voted upon, and passed unanimously.

The question was brought up as to the time and to whom the report was to be submitted. The Chairman said he understood the report was to be submitted to the President; also that recommendations along the legislative lines should be made within sixty days; that any changes of law should be recommended to the Congress so that they could be acted upon during this session. Discussion ensued as to how the report was to go to the Congress and it was decided that it ought to go as a "massive approach".

The Chairman said he would see to getting the stationery and having the names of the Committee printed down the side. He would also get the Executive Secretary and draft a letter and see to having it sent out to the organizations which Mr. Carey suggested and to any others that the members might add.

It was stated by the Chairman that it was his intention to announce the members of the three sub-committees but he doubted if the sub-committees would be able to get very much material together before the Committee as a whole met again. He would also select the Executive Secretary, and the following names were presented and considered as possibilities: Lloyd K. Garrison and Robert M. LaFollette. A discussion followed as to whether the two men would accept, which was very doubtful, and then Dr. Graham made the following motion: "That if either of these two men were available, that they be accepted". The motion was seconded, voted upon, and passed unanimously. The following alternative names were then suggested: Governor Ellis Arnall, John Pehle, Malcolm Ross, Joe Rauh, Isaac Heller, Homer Rainey, Clark Foreman, Donald Young, and James Rowe. It was suggested in the discussion that instead of getting a great name, it would be better to get a younger person who would put in a lot of time and who had ability. The person would not get much publicity and would need a great deal of energy and drive. It was also thought much better to have some one who in no way was connected with any group or organization. A motion was made by Bishop Sherrill: "That the Executive Committee be given the power to choose an Executive Secretary." It was seconded, voted upon, and passed unanimously.

The question of the date of the next meeting was then brought up. After a lengthy discussion of various dates and trying to find a time suitable for all and when the next business of the Committee would be ready to transact, it was moved, seconded, and the motion passed that the next meeting be held at 10:00 a.m. on the 5th and 6th of February. It was stated that the Executive Secretary would make all necessary arrangements and that stenographic notes of the meeting would be sent to the Committee members, who would be unable to be present, as soon as they were compiled.

A motion was made by Mr. Luckman: "That no releases or communications governing policies or purporting to express the views of the committee be made except as authorized by the Chairman. It was seconded, voted upon, and passed unanimously.

The Chairman said to send all communications which the Committee members might receive to the Executive Secretary, whose name he would give them just as soon as possible.

The meeting was adjourned at 4:00 p.m.

MINUTES OF THE MEETINGS OF THE PRESIDENT'S COMMITTEE ON CIVIL RIGHTS, FEBRUARY 5 AND 6, 1947.

Three general sessions of the President's Committee on Civil Rights were held in the conference room in the East Wing of the White House, Wednesday and Thursday, February 5 and 6. Following the adjournment of the entire committee at noon on February 6, the three subcommittees held separate meetings. In the absence of Bishop Sherrill, Mr. Matthews acted as chairman of Subcommittee No. 1. Present at the full committee sessions were: Chairman Charles E. Wilson, Mrs. Sadie T. Alexander, Mr. James B. Carey, Mr. John S. Dickey, Mr. Morris L. Ernst, Rabbi Roland B. Gittelsohn, The Most Reverend Francis J. Haas, Mr. Charles Luckman, Mr. Francis P. Matthews, Mr. Boris Shishkin, Mrs. M. E. Tilly and Dr. Channing H. Tobias.

Mr. Wilson announced the appointment of Mr. Robert K. Carr as executive secretary of the committee and Mrs. Merle Whitford as secretary to the committee. He also announced that Mr. Dickey and Mr. Roosevelt would serve with him as members of the executive committee.

Three subcommittees were announced with membership as follows:

(1) A committee to consider and determine the adequacy of existing federal legislation and to recommend proposed new legislation: The Right Reverend Henry Knox Sherrill, Ch., Francis P. Matthews, Dr. Frank P. Graham, John S. Dickey and Mrs. Sadie T. Alexander.

(2) A committee to consider the broader social, economic and educational aspects of promoting the cause of civil liberty throughout the country: Charles Luckman, Ch., The Most Reverend Francis J. Haas, James B. Carey, Channing H. Tobias and Rabbi Roland B. Gittelsohn.

(3) A committee to consider the work of private organizations whose activities affect civil rights: Morris L. Ernst, Ch., Mrs. M. E. Tilly, Boris Shishkin and Franklin D. Roosevelt, Jr.

It was voted to approve these appointments and actions.

The two sessions on February 5th were largely devoted to a discussion of the work of the subcommittees. Mr. Wilson stated that it would be helpful to the subcommittees if the entire committee could give them the benefit of its opinions on various matters at this early stage.

Subcommittee No. 1:

The work of Subcommittee No. 1 was explored at considerable length. It was thought the committee should concern itself with the following areas of possible legislative action:

(a) General Civil Rights legislation for the entire nation. Here the problem is to determine the adequacy of existing legislation, Sections 51 and 52, Title 18, the United States Code, and possibly to recommend new legislation.

(b) A specific Civil Rights Act for the District of Columbia. It was suggested in discussion that consideration of such a proposal would be advantageous for two reasons: (1) The nation's capital symbolizes the United States both to the world and to our own people. Thus it is extremely important that a satisfactory condition as to civil rights be established in Washington. (2) Such an act might serve as a model for the forty-eight states to follow in dealing with their own civil rights problems and could also be generalized and applied to the entire nation by Congress in so far as is constitutionally possible.

(c) Fair Employment Practices legislation.

(d) Anti-lynching legislation.

(e) Anti-poll tax and Election legislation.

Subcommittee No. 2:

There was less discussion concerning the work of Subcommittee No. It was suggested that this committee might study the basic social conditions and conflicts out of which civil rights violations emerge, and that it might obtain from the Gallup and Roper Polls and similar organizations information concerning group prejudices and discriminatory practices. This subcommittee would also consider ways and means of publicizing or dramatizing the work of the entire committee so as to encourage popular support for the specific recommendations which might be made in the final report.

Subcommittee No. 3:

Mr. Ernst explained at some length what he has in mind for this subcommittee. He stated that he would like to have it consider possible recommendations for legislation requiring the registration of all private organizations whose activities affect civil rights and also to require publicity as to their financial backing and their expenditures. He stated that he is interested in using the taxing and spending powers as means of forcing private and public organizations enjoying tax exemptions or government subsidies to avoid Jim Crow practices or other conduct which threatens the civil rights of individuals.

At the meeting of the entire committee the morning of February 6, Mr. Turner Smith, Chief of the Civil Rights Section of the Department of Justice, and Mr. Peyton Ford, Special Assistant to the Attorney General, were present and a discussion of the program of the Department of Justice in the civil rights field took place. Mr. Smith and Mr. Ford explained the organization of the Civil Rights Section and told of the way in which it draws upon the facilities of the entire Department of Justice in the conduct of its program. In general they felt that the present arrangement is a satisfactory one, although they admitted the Civil Rights Section could be expanded and should, perhaps, be raised to the status of a Division. There was a rather lengthy discussion about possible anti-lynching legislation and it appeared that the Department of Justice, in drafting proposed bills, has so far given its major attention to this problem.

The following miscellaneous actions were taken:

(1) It was agreed that Mr. Wilson and Mr. Carr should serve as ex officio members of the three subcommittees.

(2) It was voted that the secretariat should carry out the decision made at the first meeting of the committee to write various organizations in the civil liberties field inviting them to submit reports on their activities, and suggestions to the committee concerning its work.

(3) It was voted that the subcommittees may hold closed hearings immediately and seek the assistance of public officials or private persons and organizations, but that no subcommittee shall hold a public hearing until it has submitted a list of proposed witnesses to the entire committee and secured the latter's approval.

(4) It was agreed that the next meeting of the full committee be held on March 5 and 6 and that the subcommittees should be active in the meantime and be prepared to present progress reports at the next general meeting.

- - - - - - - - -

General Problems for Consideration of Members of the Committee:

(1) The timing and nature of public hearings, if any.

(2) The making of interim reports by the subcommittees or the committee as a whole. Should the committee hold all of its recommendations for inclusion in a final report, or should it send recommendations to the President from time to time?

(3) The time factor. It appears that recommendations pertaining to legislation should go to the President as early as possible, perhaps by the end of April. On the other hand, these will be the committee's major recommendations and there is the difficulty that later recommendations dealing with other matters might come as an anti-climax. Whatever decision is ultimately made concerning the nature of the Committee's report to the President it is clear that all phases of the work of the committee and of its subcommittees should be carried forward with the greatest possible dispatch.

Submitted by Robert K. Carr,
Executive Secretary.

Minutes of Meeting of Full Committee,
President's Committee on Civil Rights,

Wednesday morning, March 19, 1947.

The President's Committee on Civil Rights met at the offices of the Committee, 1712 G Street, at 10 o'clock, Wednesday morning, March 19. The following members were present: (1) Bishop Sherrill (who acted as chairman in the absence of Chairman Wilson and of Vice-chairmen Dickey & Dawson (1)), Dr. Tobias, Mrs. Alexander, Mrs. Tilly, Dr. Graham, Bishop Haas, Rabbi Gittelsohn, Mr. Carey and Mr. Matthews. (2)

1. Mr. Carr ~~presented~~ introduced to the Committee Mr. Milton Stewart, a new member of the research staff and two internes loaned to the Committee, Mr. Herbert Kaufman by the National Institute of Public Affairs and Joseph Murtha by the United States Government.

2. Mr. Carr then explained the pamphlet material that had been distributed to the Committee members:

<u>Action for Unity</u>, by Goodwin Watson

<u>Roots of Prejudice</u>, by Gordon Allport & Bernard M. Kramer

<u>A Declaration of Human Rights</u>, National Catholic Welfare Conference

<u>The Police and Minority Groups</u>, J. E. Weckler and Theo E. Hall

<u>Indiana State Fair Employment Act</u>

<u>Memo on George P. McNear case</u>.

3. The memorandum from Mr. Carr to Members of the Committee was considered at length. Mr. Carr read and discussed each point in the memo.

Mr. Carey felt that the section of the memo dealing with <u>Timing</u> set aside the action at the last meeting of the full Committee, March 6, when it was voted to have subcommittee reports submitted by April 15 and a Committee report of some kind by May 15. Bishop Sherrill pointed out that the recommended timing merely extended the time for subcommittees to report from April 15 to May 1 and requested a decision as to the time for a final report.

Dr. Graham moved that the date of the final report be set as October 1 rather than June 30. Rabbi Gittelsohn seconded the motion. ~~All members present except Mr. Carey voted aye. Carey voted no.~~ The motion was carried by a vote of eight to one.

Rabbi Gittelsohn made a motion that the Committee adopt as a time schedule Section E under I. in Mr. Carr's memorandum. Mrs. Tilly seconded the motion and it carried unanimously after Dr. Graham had established that it did not eliminate the previous action of the Committe (March 6 meeting) with respect to the subcommittees submitting reports April 15.

There was considerable discussion on the question of hearings or consultations with prominent people in the civil rights field appearing. Mr. Carey pointed out that if the hearings were private, much would be lost in the way of publicity. He also felt that the witnesses would be wasting valuable time to appear before only Committee members. After rather full discussion, Mr. Carey moved that people listed under II. - A. in Mr. Carr's memorandum and others suggested by Committee members be invited to appear at public hearings rather than in consultation with the Committee. Dr. Graham seconded the motion and it carried unanimously.

In a discussion about future meetings, it was agreed that the plan of having subcommittees meet on Wednesday and the full Committee on Thursday would be followed. Mr. Carr told members of the importance of notifying the staff promptly about the need for hotel reservations and also if it would not be possible for the members to attend a meeting.

Bishop Haas suggested that the Committee might wish to invite Carlos Casteneda, Professor of History at the University of Texas and an authority on problems of Spanish-American citizens in the Southwest to appear at hearings.

Mrs. Alexander felt that Houston and Marshall, both of the N.A.A.C.P. would duplicate testimony and it might be better to have only one of them and to add Arthur Garfield Hays.

Dr. Tobias suggested Mr. Lester Granger of the National Urban League.

Mrs. Tilly proposed the name of Alex Miller of the Southern Regional Office, Anti-Defamation League.

Rabbi Gittelsohn suggested John Slawson of the American Jewish Committee.

Dr. Graham listed Dr. Will Alexander of the Southern Conference on Human Welfare and Dr. Charles S. Johnson, President-elect of Fiske University. Nashville, Tenn.

Bishop Sherrill suggested Gordon Allport, co-author of Roots of Prejudice.

Dr. Graham also suggested Dr. Guy B. Johnson, Executive Director, Southern Regional Council, Atlanta, Ga.

Vol #: 2
Number: 5
Ser.: Truman Pres. Library
Collection: Tom C. Clark Papers
Box: 66
File: Pres.Cmte-Civ.Rights-'47

March 24, 1947

Mr. Milton Stewart
Research Associate
President's Committee on Civil Rights
1712 G Street, N.W.
Washington, D. C.

Dear Mr. Stewart:

In addition to the attached address of Attorney General Tom C. Clark, Tuesday, December 10, 1946, in his office at a Bill of Rights Luncheon, I am enclosing five other pieces of material that help to explain Attorney General Clark's THE FREEDOM TRAIN project. One of these pieces includes the letter from President Truman to Attorney General Clark endorsing the idea.

Cooperating with the Attorney General in this project are the following government agencies: The National Archives, The Library of Congress, The State Department, The War Department, The Treasury Department, and The United States Supreme Court.

Cooperating with the Attorney General in this project are the following private agencies: The American Heritage Foundation, especially organized to manage and finance this endeavor under the sponsorship and subject to the approval of Attorney General Clark; The Advertising Council, Inc.; The Association of American Railroads; The National Association of Manufacturers; the motion picture industry through The Motion Picture Producers Association; The American Theaters Association; and The Allied States Association of Motion Picture Exhibitors; The Periodical Publishers Association of America; The National Publishers Association; The United States Chamber of Commerce; The National Association of Broadcasters; The National Education Association; The American Bar Association; The American Bankers Association.

Helping also is Dr. A.S.W. Rosenbach, the Philadelphia antiquarian, who is contributing important documents. A long further list of individuals representing public repositories for historical documents in the various states, and patriotic, fraternal and veterans' organizations, are included among those who have already pledged their support. The nerve center for the operation of Attorney General Clark's plan is The American Heritage Foundation, whose Board of Trustees determining policy is to include Phil Murray, of the CIO; and Bill Green, of the AFL both of whom have written letters of acceptance to Attorney General Clar'

Extraordinary measures, scientific, mechanical and manual, at Attorney General Clark's direction, are being taken for the protection of THE FREEDOM TRAIN documents as they travel through the country. In this connection, the United States Marine Corps has been assigned as the armed guard by agreement between Secretary of the Navy James Forrestal and Attorney General Clark.

Please do not hesitate to call on me for any further information you may desire.

Sincerely,

WILLIAM A. COBLENZ
Assistant Director
Division of Public Information

President's Committee on Civil Rights

STANDARD FORM NO. 64

Office Memorandum • UNITED STATES GOVERNMENT

TO : The Attorney General DATE: March 24, 1947

FROM : Bill Coblenz

SUBJECT: President's Committee on Civil Rights

I understand you are to be asked to speak shortly before The President's Committee on Civil Rights. They just phoned me asking for a synopsis of THE FREEDOM TRAIN PROJECT, saying they wished to be briefed on it before you speak. I have sent them the attached resume covering specifically the points on which they asked for information.

THE PRESIDENT'S COMMITTEE ON CIVIL RIGHTS

- - - -

Washington, D. C.

April 3, 1947

WARD & PAUL
(ELECTREPORTER, INC.)
OFFICIAL REPORTERS
1760 PENNSYLVANIA AVE., N. W.
WASHINGTON 6, D. C.

NATIONAL 4266 4267 4268

Grover
aj

~~CONFIDENTIAL~~

Thursday, April 3, 1947

- - -

The President's Committee on

Civil Rights,

Washington, D. C.

The Committee met at 10:00 o'clock a.m., in the East Wing, The White House, Mr. Charles E. Wilson, Chairman, presiding.

Present: Mr. Charles E. Wilson, Mrs. M. E. Tilly, Rabbi Roland B. Gittelsohn, Mr. Charles Luckman, Mr. Francis P. Matthews, Mr. James Carey, Mr. Channing H. Tobias, Mr. John S. Dickey and Mr. Boris Shishkin.

Also present: Mr. Robert Carr, Miss Frances Williams, Mrs. Merle Whitford, Mr. John Durham, Mr. Milton Stewart, Mr. Herbert Kaufman, Mr. Joseph Murtha and Mr. Edward Jackson.

- - -

~~CONFIDENTIAL~~

CONFIDENTIAL

P R O C E E D I N G S

MR. WILSON: The Committee will please come to order.

(From 10:00 a.m. to 11:15 a.m. was devoted to a Business Session, which was not reported, and at 11:15 a.m., Hon. Tom Clark, The Attorney General of the United States arrived)

MR. WILSON: We are delighted to have you with us this morning, Mr. Clark. You got us started off on our first day and now we would like to have you enlarge on the statement you made to us then as to ~~along what lines~~ how you would like to see our efforts directed, ~~and~~ to make ~~any~~ other suggestions ~~you care to make~~ as to how you feel we can make our operations more effective along the lines that the President has laid out for us.

STATEMENT OF HON. TOM CLARK

Attorney General of the United States.

MR. CLARK: Have you come to any conclusion as to what you might beable to do from a statutory standpoint in spelling out more specifically the rights that might be secured, or have you decided that that is a Constitutional question?

MR. WILSON: I think that comes within the range of Mr. Dickey's subcommittee. Would you want to express an opinion on that, Mr. Dickey?

MR. DICKEY: I think Mr. Carr could give a better answer

CONFIDENTIAL

CONFIDENTIAL

to the question than I could, Mr. Chairman, but in so far as I have reached a personal conclusion on it - and I will let the Executive Secretary or Mr. Matthews speak for the rest of the group - I don't believe that there is an insurmountable Constitutional question there. ~~I say "insurmountable". It would not be insurmountable so far as I personally am concerned in offering the suggestion that legislation of that sort should be considered by the Congress.~~

MR. CLARK: Well, assuming that, I would say that you could render a great service by suggesting legislation that would enlarge the present Sections 51 and 52 of the Civil Rights Statutes so that those who engage in mob activity or lynching activity, as it is commonly known, might be found guilty of a Federal offense. In other words, as I outlined before, I think, the only way we can attach responsibility now under the statute is against some officer for failure to do his job or for activity in connivance with others to perform acts in violation of the statute.

The various anti-lynching bills, ~~I think, as I remember~~, are largely aimed at officials, sheriffs or constables, or people engaged in law enforcement. I think there is a responsibility likewise on the individual that engages in activity of that type. I believe that if we could attach responsi-

CONFIDENTIAL

aj CONFIDENTIAL

bility to individuals who join with others in lynching parties or mobs, you would have done a great service.

As to whether or not that ~~is a question that~~ can be solved through statutory amendment is a pretty close constitutional question, ~~as I understand it~~. Perhaps it is worth trying.

As I said, I am anxious to try to secure a case in which we can ~~[illegible]~~ extend the doctrine of Federally-secured rights to a person's right to life and his liberty and his pursuit of happiness. Under the Slaughterhouse cases those are not ~~[illegible]~~ Federally-secured rights. I am going to try to use ~~this~~ the case in South Carolina as a guinea pig, you might say. If we could extend the Federally-secured rights to include life, liberty and the pursuit of happiness, you would be able to handle a situation of this type under the existing law.

I think, too, that your Committee can spearhead interest, in localities and communities, of the responsibility of the community to prevent uprisings of this type. I think that that is most important. Law enforcement largely depends on the communities. You can't legislate morals in the people; you have to educate morals into people. We have to, ~~I think,~~ cause communities to become more interested and more public-spirited in this regard.

CONFIDENTIAL

CONFIDENTIAL

I think we have made a great advance. The other night I was studying just what had been accomplished,-and I don't mean this personally,-since I became Assistant Attorney General and head of the Criminal Division in 1943, and it is surprising that most of the cases have occurred since that time. I am speaking now of civil rights cases. ~~I don't think~~ There have been but 30 or 40 in ~~the~~ our history ~~of the States~~ that have been carried through the courts, and some 22 or 23 have been in the last four years. I think it is 25 in the last five years. So I ~~think~~ we have made great progress, and the history insofar as statistics are concerned, with reference to mob violence, shows that there has been great progress ~~been made~~ in the last two years. But I think we can make much more progress. We can insure to all groups the protection of the Federal Constitution if we can get life and liberty held to be a Federally-secured right.

I understand that you are going to make a report along that line, and I think it would be very helpful. I believe if you could interest organizations in it, ~~interest — I am not trying to name any so as to eliminate others — but~~ interest those who are public-spirited and who have a wide coverage, in trying to bring home to the American people the importance of this question, and their responsibility, you would be

CONFIDENTIAL

CONFIDENTIAL

accomplishing a great deal.

We have a Bill of Rights, you know, that we depend upon, but very few people think about a Bill of Responsibility; they don't think about that at all. They think about what "my right" is, but they don't think about "my responsibility to you." We have got to spearhead that.

Again I refer to a personal experience, but you take the juvenile problem, I think we are now getting it spearheaded and drawing attention to it. The reason I say that is every day people come in to see me about some local juvenile problem. That shows that they are becoming conscious of the problem.

[redacted] Here you have, ~~I think, just an~~ an important problem and [redacted] one that has been neglected, - one to enforce the laws, the State laws. Every time you have one of these occurrences it violates a State law, either a murder or an assault if there is not a death, and it is surprising the lack of cooperation, and in fact the refusal to cooperate, as well as a specific intent to throw obstacles in the way of investigations, that we encounter when we go in to investigate this type of case. Education is all that you can do with reference to that, I think.

I believe that Mr. Hoover talked to you, and he out ned

CONFIDE' IAL

CONFIDENTIAL

the details of the program we ~~had~~ have been following. The Department has had, [redacted], ever since Mr. Justice Murphy was the Attorney General, a Civil Rights Section [redacted] within the Criminal Division, ~~of the Department.~~ We have used the FBI as the investigative agency, as we always use it, for the purpose of/ferreting out the facts, and we have found it to be very successful. From time to time there have been some obstacles thrown in the way of the FBI, but generally we have been able to get at the facts. We have found in some communities that they just won't talk, ~~that is said,~~ like in Georgia. We had a Grand Jury down there in addition to quite a number of FBI men who had been on the job for several months, but we just couldn't get any citizens there to give us information, although we know they have it. We have, I think, two incidents down there now with reference to the treatment of a witness, a Federal witness, that may prove productive when we try them, which I hope will be next month.

In Tennessee we had a similar experience. ~~We have had similar experiences in other places.~~ Then in other communities, like in the Woodard case, although we had all the facts, the juries would turn them loose. We had a similar experience in Louisiana two weeks ago, where we had, I thought, a pretty [redacted] strong case, ~~strong case~~, but the jury turned the

CONFIDENTIAL

CONFIDENTIAL

defendants loose ~~pretty~~ very quickly.

So I think that you are going to find that education will be very helpful.

As far as the Department is concerned, we want to continue our activity, and we would like to have any suggestions that you may have. I understand that some members of the Committee are worried about the rule that Mr. Murphy put in when he was Attorney General, with reference to clearance by the Department, or the Criminal Division, of investigations before the FBI ~~could~~ can go into an investigation of a civil rights offense. That was, I think, employed and is now employed for two or three purposes. One is so that you would have a uniformity of enforcement over the United States. ~~It is a~~ There are statutes ~~that is~~ very controversial, and if we had a case down South that we did not know about in the Department, we might get a ruling that would be contrary to some case that we had in the East, ~~or something of that type~~. So we try to bring them all to the same focal point.

Second, I have used it to emphasize prosecutions. For example, in other lines of criminal activity we have authorized the FBI to take cases direct to the United States Attorneys. Then ~~all we get in the Department of Justice in Washington is the case when it is filed in the court~~ we very often don't

CONFIDENTIAL

CONFIDENTIAL

know about the investigation at all, That is handled by the United States Attorney on a local level. [redacted] We will, of course, know the progress of the case in the court, and the disposition of the case. Frankly these civil rights cases, if we handled them that way, would very often never reach the courts. We have quite a number of complaints,- I wouldn't want to venture a guess on the exact number,- but I would say it would run 10,000 a year,-on these statutes, and if we left those to local clearance I believe that you would find that we would have fewer cases than we have now.

Another reason is that of course, with that vast number of complaints, we have to [redacted] clear out the chaff from the wheat, and in doing that we try to get the stronger cases. For example, now, in our effort to extend the Federally-secured rights doctrine, if we choose [redacted] a weak case we will [redacted] lose our objective very quickly. If we choose [redacted] a strong case, we will [redacted] possibly have a better opportunity to overturn the decided cases in this field. Of course, there is only one place where we can properly evaluate ~~that we would be able to compare~~ the cases, and that is here in Washington where we [redacted] have all the cases available.

So those are some of the reasons. I don't think that there has been any delay that has caused [redacted] harm ~~to the~~ [redacted].

CONFIDENTIAL

CONFIDENTIAL

Of course, if the FBI happened to be in the vicinity at the time some occurrence came about, they would immediately go into it without any clearance at all, and then they would report it to me, as they very often do, not only in this line but in other lines, and then we would tell them to proceed. For example, in Tennessee we had a person over there before the murders were committed. The two murders were committed the day after our people got there. And in Georgia we had them there very quickly. I think you will find in most cases that expedition is the rule rather than the exception.

So I think that by bringing them here we are able to get a stronger policy. For example, in some communities, as I have said earlier, there is a tendency not to prosecute this type of case, and if we get the things here we can force them into prosecution. In the Woodward case, for example, I filed an information, or rather I requested the judge to permit us to file an information, because we felt that possibly a Grand Jury wouldn't indict. That case, aside from the national publicity incident to it, would never have come to the attention of Washington if we had not had this rule.

So while in most of these cases you will find that they do come to our attention because they are more or less publicized, the Civil Rights Section of the Department thinks

CONFIDENTIAL

and I think that it would be best to continue this clearance policy. However, I would be glad to get your reactions to it. Certainly I don't want to delay or cause any delay in the investigations of this type of case. If your study has indicated that there has been delay, I will be the first to set aside the rule, and it is within my power to do that. If there is any responsibility as to that, it is my responsibility as the Attorney General. So if you think that we should set aside the rule, I will be happy to consider that. I rather doubt if it would be best, but perhaps it would be, and I would be happy to have your reactions to it.

We also have in this Section a rule that we send out people to prosecute.. Sometimes that [redacted] a double-edged sword. In some communities there is [redacted] an inborn resentment of Washington lawyers coming in. Now we don't send a Maine lawyer to Texas to prosecute; we usually send a Texas lawyer to Texas, or a Massachusetts lawyer to Massachusetts. But we have found that it is very helpful, and the United States Attorneys generally ask for some help. We have found it helpful because the people that we send out are well acquainted with the legal end of the case, and having had a vest experience in the field they are able to get more out of a case than a United States Attorney or an Assistant United

CONFIDENTIAL

States Attorney who has handled mostly other types of prosecutions. This Section only handles this particular type of prosecution~~s~~, so they have an every-day running experience in the field which is very, very helpful. This Section has operated very successfully insofar as it has been possible to operate, and I think that an examination of their record will show that they have been not only very diligent but most conscientious in their efforts to bring about an enforcement of these particular statutes.

I have been hearing of your work and of your hearings and meetings, and I want to congratulate you and say that I am most happy to hear of the good work that you are doing. I believe that you can accomplish [a great deal] ~~considerable~~ in the field, not only in the remedial suggestions that you might make with reference ~~not only~~ to legislation but to administration, ~~but that~~ your focusing of the attention of the public on the problem will do a vast good in the advancement of the ideals that we all have, that no one is above the law and that everyone will get equal justice under the law.

If there are any questions, ~~any of you have,~~ I would be happy to attempt to answer them.

MR. WILSON: I am sure there must be questions.

MR. LUCKMAN: I would like to ask one, if I may.

CONFIDENTIAL

CONFIDENTIAL

You spoke of one instance in which you had a man actually present in an area before a murder took place. Do you feel in the Department that you have any rights, under the legislation today, to act in any way to attempt to prevent what you think may become a murder?

MR. CLARK: We very often do. For example, during the war we very often would hear of what you might call ~~call tension~~,- ~~some people call it~~ race tension,-so I would get in touch with ~~[illegible]~~ people in the various agencies - I was then Assistant Attorney General - and we would activate the agencies in the area in order to try to prevent it. For example -- ~~perhaps this should be off the record.~~

(Off the record discussion.)

MR. LUCKMAN: Under the statutes today, if you learned or had reason to believe on Tuesday that a lynching was going to take place on Wednesday, would you have the authority, for example, to move the people who you suspected were going to be lynched the next day, to another location where they might be safer?

MR. CLARK: Not unless they agreed to it.

MR. LUCKMAN: Who agreed to it, the parties involved?

MR. CLARK: Yes.

RABBI GITTELSOHN: Would you have the authority to alert

CONFIDENTIAL

CONFIDENTIAL

the FBI in that area?

MR. CLARK: I would. I ~~wouldn't say that I had~~ the authority~~, but I would do it~~. I do it many times.

I know of one or two instances where the National Association for the Advancement of Colored People has taken ~~would take~~ protective measures, ~~[illegible]~~. One was in that Louisiana case where they took two of the witnesses~~, I believe it was,~~ away so that they couldn't be bothered. They made them available to us. They have been very cooperative.

MR. MATTHEWS: If the prisoner was charged with an offense against the State statutes, would you have authority in that situation to move the prisoner for the sake of his protection against possible mob violence?

MR. CLARK: No, we wouldn't have any authority to move a prisoner unless he was in our custody.

MR. MATTHEWS: That is what I thought.

RABBI GITTELSOHN: On this matter of clearance, Mr. Clark, I think all of us recognize the need for some centralization, and as you properly presented it, the need to exert pressure from a central office on the local offices. However, some of us, at any rate, after hearing Mr. Hoover at our last meeting, were a little disturbed about the delay in getting the FBI actually on the spot for investigations. Now Mr.

CONFIDENTIAL

Hoover gave me, at least, the impression that in some cases the clearance moved so fast that he would be able to get in there and operate in 24 hours. That was given as an example of fast procedure. Now obviously, in 24 hours all kinds of clues can vanish, accidentally or otherwise. I, at any rate, ~~and I think other members of the Committee, are~~ am quite disturbed over that 24-hour to 72-hour~~, let us say,~~ possibility of evidence vanishing. Would it not be possible to preserve all the benefits of centralization by insisting on immediate reports from the field to Washington, but freeing the FBI from the requirement which they apparently are operating under now, of clearing here in Washington through the Criminal Division before they can even send investigators out to get clues before they vanish?

MR. CLARK: If Mr. Hoover thinkshe has been hampered in any way, I will correct it.

RABBI GITTELSOHN: I didn't mean to give the impression that he thought he was being hampered, but that, having heard his testimony, we wondered why it ought to take even 24 hours to get the FBI working on a case.

MR. CLARK: It shouldn't. If that is true, we ought to perhaps authorize them to make immediate investigations and reports to Washington upon the happening of any event or upon any leads that they might have, or sources that they might develop, that there would be a lynching or something of the kind. I will get together with Mr. Hoover and have that done. Certainly you are right, there might be some clues or leads destroyed in a 24-hour period, and we don't want that at all. The only purpose is to have the benefit of this central authority that we can use.

MR. TOBIAS: I was about to say that I think the Committee's Subcommittee No. 1, that is dealing with legislation, is taking into account the suggestion about Federally-secured rights. But after that has been done, and as useful as that may be, it is still true~~, it will be true,~~ that only the exceptional cases will be dealt with under such a statute, ~~when it is passed.~~ That is still the responsibility for the maintenance of law and order, and the protection of individuals under the law would be a function of the State and the local community, where the thing happens. What concerns me is that somehow or other we have to get back to the cause underlying these attacks upon particular groups of people, minority groups. I think that the chief cause is the cheapening of the personality of these groups through practices of discrimination that go unchallenged. A man is lynched because the people in the community realize that it doesn't cost as much to do him to death as it does a representative of a group whose personality is up to par. Therefore, he is the easy victim. And until he has the right of participation in local and State government to the extent that he can have some say who the officials will be, then he is going to continue to be cheap and his life is going to be taken.

Now all of that involves another responsibility of this Committee, Subcommittee No. 1, and that is the protection of people in the exercise of the franchise, and the right to become participants in government if the elective franchise is sufficient to give them that privilege.

Now the threats such as we experience in Georgia at the present time, to participation even under the declared law, declared by the Supreme Court of the United States, are such as to make all the more evident the lack of power on the part of the group concerned to protect itself, even to participate.

I don't see how we are going to be able to take care of the rank and file who are kept cheap in that way because they, as someone has expressed it, are second-class citizens. We have a double standard of personality in American life. Now that is clearly illustrated in a clipping that I took out of a paper this morning. Here in the District of Columbia a young white woman elected to go to a school that is declared - and I want to ask you whether it is true that it is declared by

CONFIDENTIAL

law - to be a Negro school in the District of Columbia. The denial of that right to her to choose the school where she feels she will get the thing that she wants, upon purely racial grounds, in the District of Columbia, ~~it seems to me~~ ~~to~~ highlights the problem not only of discrimination but the basic thing that we are talking about this morning, mob violence, because it is quite clear ~~to me~~ that mob violence results, on the scale to which we know it in America, because of these people who are below the line, below par in the acceptance of their personality.

So that it seems to me that even in order to get after the right to live and to protection from the job, we have got to get after the right of every citizen to be on equality with every other citizen in those basic rights like education, those things that involve life, like jobs, and everything of that sort; that if we are going to do a thorough job and not a superficial job, we won't just be thinking in terms of an added statute that in an emergency might take care of a situation, but of our total structure as it affects minority groups, ~~that will come up in one shape or another. For instance,~~ when ~~the South Carolina primary law is challenged,~~ ~~and I have~~ no ~~doubt that it will immediately, if the~~ veto of Mr. ~~Thompson in Georgia~~ does not hold, come up ~~there~~.

CONFIDENTIAL

CONFIDENTIAL

It isn't a direct question that I am asking; I am expressing a concern.

MR. CLARK: Yes. I think that discrimination is certainly one of the bases of the problem that you are studying, and that your conclusion with reference to trying to eliminate it [redacted] is certainly justified.

lhg

CONFIDENTIAL

MR. SHISHKIN: On this question of discrimination, General Clark, I don't know whether you have had an opportunity to give any specific thought to this, but in one of the major bills that has been introduced, the Ives-Chavez Bill of 1947, the anti-discrimination bill, there is no provision expressly dealing with discrimination in federal employment, and it presents a question that is likely to come up some time in the construction of that legislation, as to whether the federal government, in invoking a national policy on private employment, does not have a direct obligation of taking some steps to enforce that policy in its own employment. I was wondering whether you had any thoughts as to the best way in which that problem could be met - by modifying the law or by providing Executive procedure?

MR. CLARK: Frankly I don't know of any discrimination in employment in the federal government. We have attorneys of all races in our Department; we have clerks of all races; we have stenographers of all races. Some of our best attorneys happen to be colored men. I know of two or three. One was a captain in the last war, a boy named Bellinger, I believe, in the Claims Division; and then we have another who works in this very section --

MR. SHISHKIN: Well, the Department of Justice has had

CONFIDENTIAL

an excellent policy in that respect, but there has been a great deal of discrimination in federal employment elsewhere.

MR. CLARK: That could very easily be adjusted by the heads of the various departments. I don't think you need any additional legislation to accomplish that.

MR. LUCKMAN: You would lean toward an administrative solution rather than attempt to include it in current legislation?

MR. CLARK: I think you could do it much more quickly. Of course if you thought that a change of policy would occur when you had a change of executives, perhaps it would be good to put it in the legislation. However, it depends on the heads of the departments, as you well know. ~~Even though there were a statute on it, if I wanted to try to evade or avoid it, I can to some degree evade or avoid.~~ It depends after all on the individual that heads up or enfordes the partioular statute. So I think that after you got your statute it would still depend to a large extent upon the individual executive.

MR. SHISHKIN: But do you think that in the absence of a legislative enactment there would be room for an Executive order ~~enactment~~ by the President that would lay down a directive and place the responsibility on the agencies?

MR. CLARK: Well, of course President Roosevelt issued ~~had~~ such

3hg

an executive order under the War Powers Act, creating the FEPC. As to whether or not it would be necessary to have an executive order by the President in this instance, I would like to study that. I know each individual executive in each department could very easily adjust it very quickly.

RABBI GITTELSOHN: The question has come up several times, Mr. Clark, as to whether, from the point of view both of prestige and of facilitating the work itself, it might not be advisable to make of the Civil Rights Section a division in its own right, within the Department of Justice. Would you care to comment on that?

MR. CLARK: You mean have an Assistant Attorney General heading that division?

RABBI GITTELSOHN: Yes.

MR. CLARK: Well, we have six divisions in the Department now. Each usually handles a specific type of prosecution. For example, we have a Criminal Division that handles criminal cases. We have the Lands Division that handles all cases with reference to lands, condemntations and things of that type. We have the Tax Division that handles taxes. We have the Claims Division that handles claims against the Government and claims that the Government might assert itself. We have the Alien Property Division that handles all alien

4hg

CONFIDENTIAL

property. This would be a division within a division if you created a division. We have this unit ~~th[illegible]s~~ now within the Criminal Division, which ~~is autonomous in that it~~ reports to an Assistant Attorney General, but from a practcal standpoint they usually report to me. So an Assistant Attorney General would report to me likewise. I rather doubt if it would be of any assistance from the standpoint of prosecutions at all. You would have the same people doing the work. I think the matter gets down largely to the question of the individual. I believe we have in that section, ~~that unit,~~ people who are very civil-rights-minded, as we call it, and I don't believe you would be able to get any better people by having it as a separate division. You might get morepublicity from the standpoint of having an Assistant Attorney General in charge of it.

MR. TOBIAS: It would add to its prestige, don't you think?

MR. CLARK: It would do that, yes.

MR. DICKEY: Mr. Attorney General, I have at the moment some reservations as to how far we ought to go in dealing with the specific language of statutes, but that is something to be determined as we go along, and I well realize that the head of a Department is not in a position, always, to comment

CONFIDENTIAL

Shg

on specific technical questions. But do you have any opinion, ~~any personal opinion,~~ on the possibility of reaching the private participant in a lynching which arises from the victim being taken out of the hands of an officer of the law, on the basis of a rough analogy to the Lindbergh Act, by writing a federal statute based upon a showing in the hearings and in the legislative record that the great majority of the unsolved lynchings are cases where men were taken out of the hands of a state officer, and that there is a considerable social history to suggest that there was connivance on the part of the state officer in permitting his prisoner to be taken away from him? ~~and yet you find it extremely difficult to prove that?~~ Now with that legislative history behind the statute, do you have any offhand guess as to whether it would be worthwhile attempting to set up a statute to reach the private participant in such a lynching by providing that federal jurisdiction attach on the presumption, prima facie, and a rebuttable presumption, that the prisoner was taken out of the hands of the officer of the law, for the purpose of getting federal jurisdiction on there, unless within a certain period of time the state has prosecuted or indicted someone for murder - I should make it clear that that wasn't the case - or unless in the course of the trial in which that person was prosecuted, he proves that there has not been connivance with a state officer, or, as in the case of the Lindbergh Act, that he did not cross the state boundary? Have you given any thought to that? I realize that you wouldn't want to render a legal opinion on that.

MR. CLARK: Is this record going to be published?

MR. WILSON: No, this is merely for the information of the members of the Committee.

~~MR. CLARK: I just didn't want to have my offhand opinions on the law published.~~

I would say in my thought about it - and I have given considerable thought to it - that we might attach federal responsibility there on the ground that this party was deprived of a trial, that he was deprived of the right of having a jury pass on his guilt or innocence. I am speaking now of the victim. Say that the victim is in jail and all of a sudden this mob comes and takes him out. Now as you say, very often there is connivance, yet very often we are unable to prove connivance. Of course the whole problem is eliminated if we can prove connivance. Then we can handle it under the present statutes. But we will assume that we can't prove connivance and there is no question but what this mob has conspired to deprive this person of a trial which he was going to have. Say that he was in jail because he murdered somebody, or com-

7hg CONFIDENTIAL

mitted a rape. He is entitled under the Federal Constitution to a trial, and he is entitled to certain rights in that trial. I was hopeful that perhaps we might attach responsibility on that ground, and extend even the present statute, and I believe that we could certainly work out some verbiage that would amend that statute which would be helpful in the prosecution of that type of case.

What I would suggest, if it meets with your approval, is that I ask Mr. George Washington - not the Father of Our Country, but one of his successors - to collaborate with you on that. He is the Assistant Solicitor General. He and I have talked about this at length and he rather thinks that perhaps ~~there could be gotten up~~ some type of statute can be evolved that would stand the test of constitutionality.

MR. DICKEY: It seems to me that if we are to get at this lynching question, or at least at the public desire which led to the establishment of this Committee, that we have got to do more than just spell out the situation which permits you to get at the state officer who acts under color of law. Perhaps we can't get at it but it does seem to methat we have got to try to get at it if we are to meet the public desire which led to this effort.

MR. CLARK: I think the Congress may possibly create a

CONFIDENTIAL

8hg CONFIDENTIAL

right there that would come under the present Constitutional guarantees, where you would not need a Constitutional amendment. I am sure that Mr. Washington would be glad to collaborate with you with a view to getting up the verbiage of such a proposal.

MR. DICKEY: Might I ask one further question in that connection? Do you feel that this committee is going to be able to render the best help on this particular aspect of the problem by getting right down to legislative language, or do you feel that we can operate more effectively by saying that we have considered the technical aspects of this problem and we redommend the consideration of legislation in such and such a direction?

MR. CLARK: I would say that you should suggest the general plan or the general yardstick, rather than try to suggest specific legislation.

MR. DICKEY: Thank you very much.

MRS. TILLY: May I ask you a question? There are many of these lynchings that occur after a trial. What then?

MR. CLARK: You may be able to take care of that in the verbiage of your proposed statute. You mean where a person has been adjudged guilty and is either in jail or out, pending an appeal?

CONFIDENTIAL

9hg

CONFIDENTIAL

MRS. TILLEY: In such a case and also there are times when a man has been pronounced innocent, and is freed and then mobbed.

MR. CLARK: I think you will find that most of these happen before they are tried.

MR. TOBIAS: That is true.

MR. CLARK: Perhaps we could work in your suggestion, Mr. Dickey, along with these others.

MR. DICKEY: I realize that ~~you have the other approach~~ there.

MR. CLARK: We should use all the avenues, all the things we have, to bolster up our statute, and we would use them, of course. ~~That does pose a problem which in some instances would be true.~~

MR. CAREY: What rights are accorded an American national travelling outside the boundaries of our country; what protection is accorded him by the Federal Government?

MR. CLARK: ~~Well, just~~ the usual protections of international law. We would protest to the other government if anything happened to one of our nationals. We don't have any police powers in those other countries.

MR. CAREY: Could we hold that government responsible?

MR. CLARK: Yes.

CONFIDENTIAL

10hg

CONFIDENTIAL

MR. CAREY: Couldn't we develop something, along the lines that have been suggested, that citizens of this country should be accorded at least the same rights and privileges and protection, travelling or maintaining themselves in this country, that our federal government accords our nationals when they are travelling outside our boundaries?

MR. CLARK: Well, I think that is largely dependent upon diplomatic relations, and international law. For example, if I were travelling in England and murdered somebody, I expect I would get pretty summary punishment, assuming I was not the Attorney General.

But I think that is a suggestion we ought to look into. However, I think we have stronger grounds on which to base it. If you will study the trends of the decisions I believe you will find that there is a pretty good chance of prevailing, at the present time.

MR. CAREY: I am thinking in terms of the tremendous national appeal that existed say in the recent shooting down of some of our fellows in Yugoslavia. There was more excitement over that and more action by the federal government than is indicated when citizens of this country are lynched right here within our own boundaries.

MR. CLARK: Of course they were soldiers of the United

CONFIDENTIAL

11hg CONFIDENTIAL

States, and that is somewhat different.

MR. LUCKMAN: It puts them in a different classification.

MR. CLARK: Yes.

MR. CAREY: I think the difference runs the other way. One is a peaceful citizen and the other is part of the armed forces. I am just thinking of the political aspects of it. I think that we should have at least as much, or more interest in the human life right here at home. We should have more control and greater ability to protect a citizen here than we would elsewhere.

MR. CLARK: We do.

MR. CAREY: I am thinking in terms of the federal government providing adequate opportunity for a local administration to protect its citizens, but failing to do so the federal government would have reason to expect some accounting for acts of violence against its citizens.

MR. CLARK: Don't you think that conditional statutes are unsatisfactory? I wouldn't condition it on local action. I would just ~~flat-footedly~~ flatly say that anyone who engages in this type of activity is guilty of a federal offense. If the state wants to move in there first, all right, let them do it. We have many statutes now that overlap, state and federal. ~~and we don't prosecute them when the state does in many cases.~~ For

CONFIDENTIAL

12hg CONFIDENTIAL

example, in the case of gambling and things of that type, the state very often handles that, or sometimes we might handle it, for example on a federal reservation, ~~or something like that.~~ Or, if we have a man who has been convicted and has received a shorter sentence than we think he possibly should have received, and he has committed some stateoffense and the state asks us to release him, we very often do that for state prosecution. But I believe you are going to ~~couch~~ place your statute in very grave doubts when you make it conditioned on the activity or inactivity ~~on the part~~ of a state, because that is a question itself. Suppose the state moves in tomorrow morning and returns a "no bill" from a grand jury. That is what they will do. Then your whole federal statute is stricken down by these 16 men that are on this state grand jury, or 23 men, or whatever number they have on it - most of them have 16.

So I think myself we ought to make it just an affirmative offense against [redacted] the United States. Then you have got the human element of an Attorney General of the United States, and a District Attorney or Attorney General of a State - and we usually get along fine, I don't know of any with whom I don't get along - and if they move in diligently and sincerely, -- [redacted] we have got enough prosecutions,

CONFIDENTIAL

13hg

CONFIDENTIAL

~~I don't want any more if I can keep from it.~~ -- I would rather do it on a local level because it would do more good on the local level than on the national basis. If you can get the local law enforcement officers to act quickly and diligently and sincerely, you can do much more good, and it builds up the community, and that is what I want to see done.

At the same time I wouldn't want to have my action depend upon some activity of a local officer because you are going to find that there is many a slip there, and it might look as if there was a lot of activity but there might not be any sincerity in it.

MR. SHISHKIN: Our subcommittee has been exploring the problem of the sources of ~~activities~~ support of some organizations that have been spreading hate and intolerance, and considering the problem of the possibility of reaching at the sources of their operation, ~~and one of those - I mean dealing with the spending and taxing powers of the federal government in application to such private organizations -~~ and I was just wondering what your reaction in general would be to the denial of tax exemption to organizations that are placed by statute into a category of that kind, however the category is defined?

MR. CLARK: Well, I hadn't thought about it, but as a

CONFIDENTIAL

14hg

general rule I don't believe in indirection, I believe in direction. You are trying to do something indirectly that you should do directly. I would like to go off the record.

(Discussion off the record)

RABBI GITTELSOHN: On that loyalty executive order there is some reason to feel that the civil rights of federal employees may be endangered by that order. Would you have any comments or suggestions to make as to how we can on the one hand protect the Government against disloyalty, and on the other hand not subject federal employees to the kind of witch hunt which would be clearly a violation of their own civil rights?

MR. CLARK: ~~Well, perhaps~~ There won't be any witch hunt. Certainly any power that I have will be used to prevent a witch hunt.

There are three things in the order, I think, that would protect that. One would be with reference to the organizations that an employee should not belong to, like the Communist Party or some such organization as that, The Attorney General is supposed to declare whether or not those organizations are subversive, and if they are that is a ground for the removal of the employee who belongs. There we have to use very careful discretion; we have to be certain that the organizations that we do declare subversive are actually subversive,

15hg CONFIDENTIAL

and we should use the same amount of proof in that regard as we would in a courthouse when we ~~go~~ to determine whether or not a man is guilty.

In the second place, with reference to your various government documents that the Joint Intelligence Staff has a right to designate as being Secret or Non-Secret, I think they have to use a little ~~bit~~ more discretion than they did~~, perhaps,~~ during the war when they just had a stamp that said Confidential, or Secret or Super-Secret, or something like that. But your protection would be in the head of the department. We don't take away, in this order, the responsibility ~~f~~or the authority of the head of the department. When the Congress passes an appropriations act appropriating to the Department of Justice $100,000,000 ~~to run the Department.~~ it is up to the Attorney General to see that that is properly expended, and that the Department is properly operated. So this order recognizes that and so, when it came up to him to determine whether a ~~party~~ man wasnot loyal to the United States, he would consider these various factors - just what organization the ~~party~~ man belonged to, and if the Attorney General had determined it to be subversive, ~~what his adherence to those principles were with reference to this particular employee~~. If it involved documents of the Government, the type of docu-

CONFIDENTIAL

16hg CONFIDENTIAL

ments and just what they were. And then, on top of that, if he decides against the employee, the employee can go to the Civil Service Board and get a recommendation from it. It still preserves, however, the authority and the responsibility - that is the main thing - of the head of the department. If you don't do that a man can't run his department. You have to give him authority and you have to place the responsibility ~~somewhere.~~ on him.

I know that soon after I became Attorney General it was suggested to me that we admit error in a case down here that the Supreme Court decided some two weeks ago, with reference to a New York lawyer. And I said no, that I thought we ought to carry it on through and just see the pattern, see just what activity we could take, what the Court would say about it. And we took it up and the Court of Appeals decided it here in the District, gave us a yardstick to go by.

So I don't think you need to worry about any witch hunts or any persecution under the order. I think, myself - and I am quite sure that a number of you think - that there has been perhaps a little too much hullabaloo, [redacted], about the Communists ~~and about the~~ and subversive activities, ~~partic-~~ [redacted]y in Government. Frankly the reports that I get - and I get hundreds of them from the FBI and other agencies, in-

CONFIDENTIAL

17hg telligence services - indicate that in comparison to the number of employees in the Government there is a very, very small percentage that even have any subversive tendency, much less belong to Communistic or Fascist organizations.

(At this point Mr. Shishkin asked a question off the record, and the answer thereto, and the following discussion was also requested to be off the record).

MR. WILSON: General, thank you very much; it has been tremendously helpful and a real pleasure to have you with us.

MR. CLARK: I am glad to have been here and I hope you will feel free to call on me at any time that you feel I may be of assistance to you.

- - -

(Adjournment at 12:45 p.m. to 2:00 p.m. of the same day)

- - -

CONFIDENTIAL

2:00 p. m.

MR. WILSON: Ladies and gentlemen, we are very happy to have Professor Robert E. Cushman, Professor of Government at Cornell. We are delighted to have you come, Professor, and talk to us on this subject, which, as you know, we have been studying for some time; and we would be happy to have you make a statement, and we would like to have the privilege of asking you some questions at the conclusion of your statement.

STATEMENT OF PROFESSOR ROBERT E. CUSHMAN,

PROFESSOR OF GOVERNMENT, CORNELL UNIVERSITY.

PROF. CUSHMAN: Mr. Chairman and members of the Committee, as you know, I am a teacher by trade; so if my statement sounds like a classroom lecture, that is the result of an occupational disease, and you will have to overlook it.

I want to make five points or comment on five different things in connection with your program, about which I know something in a rather general way through my previous association with your secretary, Mr. Carr.

My first point is that it seems to me that one of the responsibilities and opportunities of a Committee like this is to clarify and emphasize the constitutional limits upon the power of the Federal Government to protect individual civil rights. I think there is a tremendous amount of confusion of

CONFIDENTIAL

CONFIDENTIAL

mind on that point, evidenced by the steady stream of demands that Congress do things which it quite obviously does not have the constitutional authority to do.

Most of us, I think, tend a little to keep active in our thinking the old Theodore Roosevelt doctrine of new nationalism, that there ought to be a Federal power adequate to deal with any purely national problem, whether the Constitution has put it there or not.

Well, unfortunately -- or fortunately, whichever way you happen to look at it -- that doesn't happen to be good constitutional law; but most people are not aware of the fact that it isn't. They can't understand why these problems are not met by a head-on drive upon the part of the Federal Government.

I was impressed by that in reading the accounts of the FBI investigation of this lynching down in Monroe County, Georgia, last summer. I suppose it would be fair to say that nine out of ten people who read the accounts and read that the FBI was investigating that lynching went on from there to the easy and somewhat natural assumption that if the culprits were caught, the Federal Government do something about it directly and expeditiously, having no clear idea of the narrow legal basis on which the Department of Justice has to proceed under Section 52 of the Code.

CONFIDENTIAL

CONFIDENTIAL

I think, to sum it up, it is of very great importance that we get as many people to understand that there is a division of labor/in our Federal system of government between the National Government and the States and that the National Government's powers in this are are as limited as they are.

Point No. 2 -- I think that your Committee should propose and strongly defend improvements in and strengthening of the existing civil rights statutes dealing particularly with matter which are safely within the recognized area of Federal power.

I gather from the President's Executive Order setting up the Committee that that was one of the rather specific things that it was supposed that the Committee would undertake to do. I don't see how this can be very seriously controversial. I have checked over the field to the extent to which I am familiar with it; the things that occur to me concretely are the improvements, supplementing Section 52 of the present Code, especially improvements which would eliminate the rather awkward limit on Federal power which resulted from the court's emphasis in the Screws case on the element of a wilful intent to abridge civil rights in the case of an indictment brought under Section 52.

There ought to be, I should suppose, an increase in the penalty attached to that statute; and perhaps, a general clarification and amplication of it.

CONFIDENTIAL

CONFIDENTIAL

It seems to me in the second place, the second point at which improvement is indicated lies in the area of sharpening and pointing up the statutes which deal with both private and official invasion of the right to vote, particularly in Federal elections, but in State elections in so far as Federal power extends into that field; and the principal implementation which seems to me to be needed there is to give the Department of Justice authority or power to go into court and get injunctive relief against invasion of the right to vote in advance, and possibly the right to proceed under the Federal declaratory judgment Act in suitable cases. Also ~~probably~~ some clarification of the status of primary elections is needed.

I have not been able to persuade myself, as a student of constitutional law for many years, that much, if anything, in the way of concrete legislation can be made to hinge on the republican form of government guarantee in the Federal Constitution. Maybe some of the lawyers present would disagree with that, but I think that is a rather frail foundation for anything substantive.

Finally, I gather that the very rarely used section of the Code dealing with slavery needs some modernization to give it adequate coverage; but in that general area I should think there ought to be no serious difficulty in providing at

CONFIDENTIAL

J5

CONFIDENTIAL

least some further aid to the Department of Justice in more effective enforcement of the laws that they now have at their disposal.

Point No. 3 brings me to a whole series of highly controversial proposals for Federal legislation aiming to protect quite a wide range of civil rights. Here are the proposals with regard to lynching, Federal FEPC, a code of civil rights for the District of Columbia, anti-Jim Crow law affecting interstate transportation, an anti-poll tax law, and quite a variety of others that could be put into that category. Some of these seem to me to be controversial because of rather serious constitutional doubts as to the authority of Congress at present to legislate with respect to them in any very effective and direct way.

A good many of them are politically highly controversial. They aren't as far as I am concerned. I think I am in favor of every one of them so far as the policy and content goes, although I do have a good deal of doubt about the constitutionality of one or two of them.

I hadn't planned to discuss those because it seemed to me that the extent to which a Committee of this kind is likely to get into the consideration of them is going to involve a number of problems of strategy with which an outsider can hardly be

CONFIDENTIAL

J6

CONFIDENTIAL

familiar. I don't mind saying that I am a good deal of a realist about these things. I think that some of these things are politically impossible in any manageable period of time in the immediate future.

I am not sure that it wouldn't be my judgment that it would be unfortunate to propose in a definite and immediate way a good deal more than there was any chance of getting and thereby lose what seems to me to be pretty well within the reach of the Committee; but there again I feel I am talking about things that one outside your circle is not equipped to discuss with any thoroughness.

The fourth point, and in my judgment a point which I think is a vitally important point, is this: A Committee on Civil Rights set up by the President of the United States has a unique opportunity to focus the attention of the American people on the fundamental importance and value of our American rights and freedoms. I don't mean by that merely the little narrow list of things about which Congress can legislate. I mean the whole American tradition of civil liberty in all of its aspects.

The reason I feel so strongly about the importance of this particular aspect of the opportunity that seems to me to be yours is that I am convinced that there is an intimate and

CONFIDENTIAL

CONFIDENTIAL

inescapable connection between the preservation of rights and freedoms in this country and an intelligent public opinion. If you don't have a community opinion which supports laws or the administration of laws devoted to the protection of civil liberty, in the long run civil liberty is not going to be adequately and satisfactorily protected.

On the other hand, if you don't have civil liberty, you aren't going to have any mechanism by which you can hope to get a public opinion which amounts to anything -- so that the two things are bound up together.

I have felt for a long time and continue to feel very strongly that those of us who are not members of minority groups and who, perhaps, have no special axes to grind, ~~a very large~~ number ~~of people who don't feel the pressure at any time of~~ any conceivable invasion of ~~civil liberties -- that group~~ lose track of the fact that we have a tremendous social stake in the preservation of the American code of rights and freedoms. We tend to~~, I think,~~ associate civil liberties and civil rights, the very terms, with minority groups, with people who are being pushed around for some reason or another, and very often people with whom we ourselves do not agree and perhaps aren't particularly keen on being associated with.

Furthermore, we have left in the main to the minority

CONFIDENTIAL

CONFIDENTIAL

groups and the crusading organizations as much of the job as has been done of educating the American people about American rights and freedoms. We get very little of it on any other level.

I think there is a great distortion of judgment about the problem, which has resulted from that; which is why I feel so strongly the advantage of having the prestige of the United States Government somehow associated with a problem of this kind. I thought when the Civil Rights Section was set up in the Department of Justice that just the fact that it was set up was of great importance, irrespective of what it accomplished.

I thought when this Committee was created, that again was an item in the building up of prestige and the focusing of national attention upon problems that everybody ought to have an interest in. Your report will accomplish a great deal in that regard.

It is very interesting to observe that the Supreme Court in a series of decisions in the past seven or eight years has been moving along until it now occupies squarely the position that the civil liberties guaranteed by the first amendment to the Constitution of the United States -- freedom of religion, press, speech, assembly -- are in a preferred position in our constitutional scheme of values, that they are of deeper and more vital importance than other clauses of the Constitution.

CONFIDENTIAL

So that if a law is passed which appears on its face to abridge any of them, the presumption is no longer in favor of the validity of the law; the presumption is against the validity of the law until it can be shown that there is a clear and present danger which justifies it.

What it adds up to is that the Court, at least, has moved into this position of recognizing the very high importance of these rights and liberties which form part of the American tradition. I think just for purposes of pure propaganda in dealing with governments which are not democratic governments, as the Soviet Union, we can't possibly overemphasize the extent to which we are bound to defend the civil liberties which form the basis of democratic government in this country.

I think this Committee has an opportunity it certainly ought not to lose -- and I am pretty confident it won't lose -- in just registering its own conviction of the importance of this whole area.

That leads me to my final point, which is that I very much hope that out of your deliberations there may come a proposal for some sort of a continuing organization on a national level, to which would be confided, perhaps, a somewhat general responsibility as an advisory agency to keep attention focused on American rights and freedoms, to keep on capitalizing the

j10

CONFIDENTIAL

prestige of the Federal Government as being actively interested in seeing that the people of this country understand what those rights and freedoms are and how important they are to the continuation of the democratic process.

I could conceive that a council or committee or some sort of organization, perhaps a civilian group operating through a paid staff, could keep going a set of interests and activities which would not subject them to criticism as taking sides in any particular controversy, but which would serve as a clearing house of information, an agency which might organize from time to time public conferences of leaders of thought in various fields connected with the general problem and which might conceivably carry on, perhaps, a certain amount of research either on its own or in connection with some of the research agencies here in Washington which are equipped to make studies on particular problems.

That is about the substance, Mr. Chairman, of what I have to say. It is not very impressive, but it summarizes my own immediate thoughts, at least, with regard to what I conceive to be your assignment and what you might possibly be trying to make out of it.

MR. WILSON: That is a very excellent exposition, Professor Cushman, and very helpful; and I am delighted that we

CONFIDENTIAL

CONFIDENTIAL

have the record of it because I think it will be very helpful as we attempt to carry out this job which you have outlined.

I think, generally speaking, the Committee will find itself very much in agreement with what you had to say.

Now, have you questions for Professor Cushman?

MR. LUCKMAN: I have one, Professor Cushman, which I simply did not understand the meaning of. When you were listing the individual suggestions, I think under Point 3 you spoke of an anti-Jim Crow law affecting interstate commission?

PROF. CUSHMAN: Transportation. The follow-up of ~~them~~ the Morgan Case.

MR. LUCKMAN: Yes.

RABBI GITTLESOHN: You mentioned the Supreme Court restriction by interpretation of what was probably the original intent of [redacted] of the post Civil War civil rights legislation.

Would you care to venture an opinion on what the prospects or chances would be of a more liberal Supreme Court interpretation if new civil rights legislation of that type were written and, of course, eventually came before the Supreme Court for a test of constitutionality? Do you think the change in the complexion of the Court in recent years would have any great effect on their interpretation of such laws?

CONFIDENTIAL

CONFIDENTIAL

PROF. CUSHMAN: I don't know that I have any clear opinion about that. The point was a technical one and I think there is some reason to believe that the opinion which the Court wrote in the Screws case, which injected this pretty unworkable element into the picture of insisting that a jury be charged that if Jones beat Smith over the head, if he is an officer of the law, he must have had in mind when he beat him that he was violating his civil liberties or civil rights instead of just trying to beat him.

That makes it pretty difficult to do any business there. Well, the impression that I have is that what you got out of that was something of a compromise among members of the Court, ~~and by gaining that much~~ by which the Court avoided holding the statute inapplicable altogether.

~~I wouldn't want to go to bat on that, but that I have heard rumored around. I don't know of any possible way of anticipating what the Court would do with a new statute.~~

The word "wilful" is in the statute. It would be easy to take it out and see what you had left if you went into court
3- on it, and you probably wouldn't know until you did. There is a disposition on the part, I think, of some of the Justices to keep in mind all the while that penetration of Federal authority into an area traditionally occupied by the States, and

CONFIDENTIAL

CONFIDENTIAL

particularly in the field of the enforcement by the States of State law, is something that should move pretty slowly. I don't think the orthodox judicial slant on that is very friendly, S. ~~to it.~~

Nevertheless, I would expect most of these specific changes which have been suggested in the present statutes to be upheld. The Court went pretty far in the Primary Cases, of course.

MR. TOBIAS: You spoke of what I think Cavour referred to as an enthusiasm for the possible. Take, for instance, the situation in the District of Columbia, the segregation policy here, which from some points of view would be politically impossible of eradication; yet it is just that kind of thing that makes it impossible for us to refer with emphasis in the working of our system, particularly when we have in mind certain governments of different ideology -- I think it is important, and my whole enthusiasm for the work of this Committee is that it shall lift American prestige in the world, which these practices are making it impossible to do.

It will be a difficult thing to bring about a change, for instance, in the segregated public school system of the District of Columbia, but it is a standing reflection on our American democracy that we have adopted in the nation's capital

CONFIDENTIAL

the least desirable pattern of education. It seems to me that even though that might be classified among the politically impossible things, that we ought to have an enthusiasm for it, anyhow.

PROFESSOR CUSHMAN: I am not sure I wouldn't go along with you on that particular issue, partly because I don't think that it would have the same kind of ramifications that a frontal attack on a nation-wide scale might have. Of course, there is nothing that I resent so much in this whole field as the fact that this is a Jim Crow town. It just burns me up.

What I had in the back of my mind was that, as you say, you quote Cavour -- I usually quote Burke, who told the House of Commons once:

"I hope I shall never fail to do a proper thing because there is something else more proper which I am unable to do."

That is a reasonably sound practical bit of philosophy. In any event, I was merely drawing attention to the fact that it is possible for a set of proposals to get into a context where you just are going to have them scrapped.

I was a member of the staff of the Brownlow Committee, the President's Committee on Administrative Management, back in 1936. When that job was done, I am firmly convinced that Congress would have passed most of that program. Very little

CONFIDENTIAL

of it was controversial on any serious basis. Mr. Hoover, Governor Lowden, Mr. Landon had all promised to come and testify before the appropriate committee. Two weeks later the President sent his Supreme Court proposal to Congress. When that fight was over, he couldn't have gotten the reorganization of the National Screw Thread Commission out of Congress. The whole thing was just wrecked by being associated with something else which had been resented.

Now, maybe that is a philosophy of timidity, and I am not expressing a judgment about it. Frankly, I don't know what I would do if I had responsibility in a matter of this kind. I don't think the Committee ought to ignore these issues. Whether it should make specific proposals for immediate action would be a matter that would seem to me would be one of the most difficult problems you would have to deal with. To simply say this law ought to be passed right away -- maybe it should be.

RABBI GITTLESOHN: What are some of the things you feel are politically impossible on the list you gave us? You said some of them are politically impossible.

PROFESSOR CUSHMAN: Maybe none of them are. I don't know whether a national FEPC is or not. I think that is getting into the general field where it is within possible shooting

CONFIDENTIAL

CONFIDENTIAL

distance of your getting a kind of support for it which you didn't previously have. Of course, I think the anti-poll tax legislation is ~~thoroughly bad~~ questionable. I happen to be one of the constitutional lawyers that has very grave doubts about the constitutional power of Congress to legislate poll taxes out of existence. And the same about any thorough-going anti-lynching statute. I think you can go part way in dealing with lynching. You can improve the legislation with which you deal with conspiracies and mob violence, if you can draw in some officer.

I don't think there is any sound footing for an anti-lynching statute which simply moves in and makes it a Federal crime to kill somebody by lynching him. That is my own opinion.

MR. SHISHKIN: A~~part from the political concern, there are two phases to this question with regard to the political limitations, and~~ As to the constitutional doubts, you feel that the anti-lynching and anti-poll tax statutes are the ones about which there might be ~~unconstitutional~~ doubt?

PROFESSOR CUSHMAN: Yes.

MR. SHISHKIN: I think it is important for our Committee to know the limitation.

PROFESSOR CUSHMAN: I don't think there can be any serious

CONFIDENTIAL

doubt about the constitutionality of a properly drawn FEPC statute based on the commerce clause. I mean if the Fair Labor Standards Act is good constitutional law, I don't see why the basis of objectionable employment conditions shouldn't be extended, if Congress wishes to extend it, ~~and~~ Certainly the Congress has full authority over the District of Columbia, ~~and~~ If Congress wishes to establish a policy of non-segregation on all interstate carriers, there can't be the slightest doubt about its authority to do so. That would be my feeling.

Those two are, in my judgment, dubious. I hasten to say that lawyers in whose judgment I have very great confidence disagree with me about that, so maybe it is worthwhile to try them out and see what you can get out of the Supreme Court in order to be sure.

~~MR. LUCKMAN: That is one thing you can be sure of?~~

~~PROFESSOR CUSHMAN: Yes.~~

MR. SHISHKIN: What is your feeling with respect to the proposal for a Federal law that would require private organizations whose activities might affect civil rights of citizens to disclose the sources of their financial backing?

PROFESSOR CUSHMAN: I am in favor of it. I am in favor in general of this general policy of disclosure all along the line. ~~Probably a lot of organizations that haven't anything~~

~~to do with civil liberties~~ My reason for feeling as I do is that if you think about the process of forming a public opinion in this country at the present time, you can no longer think of it in terms of Holmes' epigram about truth competing against falsehood in the market place.

You have these propaganda organizations, and a good public relations man will tell you if you will pay him a certain amount of money, he will sell any idea to the American people that you want to buy and have presented to them.

In a context of that kind, how are you going to get any protection ~~to~~ of the integrity of a public opinion emerging from ~~that~~ the clash of highly charged propaganda campaigns? Well, maybe the disclosure of who is paying for them and what is back of the organization that is putting the campaign across may not be too useful, but it is a little help. After all, if you do know who is paying for an onslaught on the public eye and ear and what sort of an organization it is, that at least helps you make up your mind as to whether it is a crowd you want to go along with or whether you don't.

I can't myself see any reason why one should seriously object to it. I realize that many organizations do, but on the whole I feel that we are bound to come to it sooner or later just in self-protection, just in order to know where these ideas

CONFIDENTIAL

come from, which we know somebody is paying somebody a lot of money to disseminate.

The American Civil Liberties Union, I gather -- I have had some correspondence with Roger Baldwin about that -- ~~I~~ ~~think they are~~ divided, ~~their ranks are pretty badly divided~~ on that point, but my own opinion is very firm on it.

DR. DICKEY: If you did have responsibility and you had to choose where you were going to throw your effort, where would you throw your effort in this whole field of civil rights?

PROFESSOR CUSHMAN: You mean from the standpoint of looking at it as a member of this Committee or just in general?

DR. DICKEY: Well, to make it easy, as a member of this Committee -- or to make it difficult, perhaps. I am very much impressed with what you say myself that we may have to choose here in emphasis as to what needs doing most first.

PROFESSOR CUSHMAN: Well, I think -- without repeating myself -- I think that certainly there couldn't be any question about the proposal of improvements in the existing legislation. I can't see that anybody could object to that.

DR. DICKEY: You mean attempting to meet the difficulties of the Screws case? That would be a pretty small mouse to turn this Commission loose on, would it not?

PROFESSOR CUSHMAN: Yes, maybe so, but certainly that much--

CONFIDENTIAL

there wouldn't be any disagreement that that ought to be part of your program. At least, that would be my feeling about it.

I confess that I feel the educational potential in this is as important as anything you are likely to do. I mean if the thing could be implemented satisfactorily, it seems to me that the presentation of a report that focused attention on the whole broad field, whether you came out flatfootedly in favor of a particular statute~~, civil rights statute~~ or not, the emphasis on the general importance of broadening the information of the American people about these subjects and the intention of trying to see that that was kept going seems to me to have more possibility of paying dividends than almost anything else you can do.

I don't think Congress is going to pass an FEPC statute because your Committee commends it.

I have no objection to your recommending it, and I hope Congress will pass it, but my own feeling is that to get national attention focused on some of these problems is of very great importance.

DR. DICKEY: Do you think that a civil rights statute for the District of Columbia would stand as high as any other vehicle in importance that we might use to focus national attention on these questions?

CONFIDENTIAL

PROFESSOR CUSHMAN: I thinkyou are probably right. Yes, I think so.

DR. DICKEY: Of course, that leads you, I suppose, right into the suffrage issue, doesn't it?

~~PROFESSOR CUSHMAN: Yes.~~

~~MR. WILSON: Leads into what?~~

~~DR. DICKEY: Suffrage.~~

~~MR. WILSON: Oh, yes?~~

PROFESSOR CUSHMAN: I am not sure that I know just what you have in mind there. ~~Of course, on the suffrage issue, I think the present civil rights statutes do need some further implementing and revision in order to stiffen up what the Department of Justice can do in the existing area which it now occupies. If you have in mind --~~

DR. DICKEY: I had in mind the suffrage problem in the District of Columbia primarily.

~~PROFESSOR CUSHMAN: I am not too sure I know exactly what it is.--~~

~~DR. DICKEY: That is, the District does not have a vote.~~

PROFESSOR CUSHMAN: Yes, yes, [redacted] of course. I was thinking in terms of Negro suffrage in surrounding territory.

Of course, I have never been able to understand exactly why the District of Columbia shouldn't have suffrage on some

CONFIDENTIAL

basis or other. I don't know why it shouldn't be a point that a Committee like this might well consider.

DR. DICKEY: We have been told by some that you won't get civil rights in the District until you get suffrage for everyone. Then, on the other hand, we are told by others that if you get suffrage for all, you can just put it down you are not going to get civil rights.

PROFESSOR CUSHMAN: I hadn't been thinking about that particular problem in this context at all. I think it probably belongs here, however.

RABBI GITTLESOHN; Dr. Cushman, I am very much interested personally in your suggestion that we try to make this a continuing effort rather than let it die with the expiration of this Committee. I think all of us are pretty well convinced by now that at best we will be able to touch only a small segment of the total problem.

Do you think the pattern of the White House Conference for Children, for example, might be fruitful for a continuation of this kind of work on a similar basis?

PROFESSOR CUSHMAN: I am not familiar with the detail of that, but something of that sort -- I hadn't really thought the thing through in my own mind.

It would seem to me it ought not to be a governmental

CONFIDENTIAL

enterprise, or such as ~~[illegible]~~ another bureau or office. ~~part of the United States Government.~~ As soon as you give it that status, you would rob it of a very large part of any influence it might have.

RABBI GITTLESOHN: But it should have government sponsorship?

PROFESSOR CUSHMAN: Yes, by all means, but it ought to be composed of a representative group. There should be drawn into it planning and management, a representative group of distinguished citizens such as such a group as this, probably not as large as this if it were to be a continuous working agency.

Perhaps the results would be a bit intangible, but there are a lot of things that could be done. The lack of understanding in this area is really appalling, and we are tending to lose civil rights simply because people no longer appreciate that they have existed and are worth doing anything about. While I don't think the Government can engage in propaganda, it can engage in an educational program on a dignified level, which would seem to me to produce results.

MR. SHISHKIN: Professor Cushman, there was one point that was brought out in some of our discussions with respect to restrictive covenants, particularly that phase of it where the restrictive convenant might be used as a device to support the price of the property or enhance the value of the property

CONFIDENTIAL

CONFIDENTIAL

through conspiratorial methods. Perhaps there is a further limitation on the area we could reach by directing it to the point where the holdings might be large and might have interstate aspects, such as insurance companies or banks or other large holders; but starting at this easy point of that limited application, do you think anything might be done by reaching it through the anti-trust laws technique?

~~PROFESSOR CUSHMAN: You mean here in the District?~~

~~MR. SHISHKIN: I meant nationally.~~

PROFESSOR CUSHMAN: I hadn't thought of it. I hadn't supposed that these convenants were of such scope that they could be brought within any sphere of interstatecommerce.

MR. SHISHKIN: Only in so far as large holdings were concerned, but there are situations which might be placed within the area of monopolistic practice involving real estate, and I was just wondering whether you thought that was beyond our reach completely or whether there might be some means of dealing with it federally.

PROFESSOR CUSHMAN: It is not a problem that I know anything particularly about. It doesn't offhand seem to me to be very promising, but there might be something in it that I don't see.

MR. CARR: One other matter that has come up again and

CONFIDENTIAL

CONFIDENTIAL

again is the use of the taxing and spending powers to withhold subsidies or tax exemption privileges from organizations, public or private, ~~who~~ which practice discrimination or in other ways threaten civil rights.

How promising an approach does that seem to you to be?

PROFESSOR CUSHMAN: Well, there is certainly a potential weapon there. We will know a little more about it, perhaps, in another year or so in New York. We have been having a battle up there for quite a little while, trying to get some legislation like that through the New York State legislature. I don't believe it passed.

MR. TOBIAS: No.

PROFESSOR CUSHMAN: I am not too convinced that a great deal is likely to be accomplished by that method, ~~but~~ for it is very difficult to enforce, as the New York experience seems to indicate.

Of course, theoretically we have a statute in New York which would seem to be adequate to deal with that problem, but when it comes to picking out the institutions in New York that receive tax exemptions and are discriminating on the basis of race or creed, nobody seems to be able to pin anything on anybody in particular. That is the general impression.

If you tried to do that on a national level -- there is

CONFIDENTIAL

CONFIDENTIAL

unquestionably a weapon there. I am not sure it isn't a back-handed way of coming at the problem, but it might be useful to experiment with it.

MR. WILSON: If it could be made to work, it would be a truly effective way.

PROFESSOR CUSHMAN: Yes.

MR. WILSON: Because it would cover so much ground.

PROFESSOR CUSHMAN: Yes.

MR. WILSON: The use of Federal funds or Federal funds withheld.

DR. DICKEY: The New York legislation that you refer to--- does that relate to withholding of State funds?

PROFESSOR CUSHMAN: Tax exemption. I think it is a fairly old statute.

DR. DICKEY: Property or income? Income tax?

PROFESSOR CUSHMAN: Property. I don't think these institutions would pay any income tax.

DR. DICKEY: I was thinking of contributions by an individual to the institution.

PROFESSOR CUSHMAN: Merely an assessment on the real estate

RABBI GITTLESOHN: That is right.

MR. WILSON: In New York State, if I am not mistaken, in institutions -- we will just call it an orphanage as an

CONFIDENTIAL

17

example -- if it is going to get State funds, it can not discriminate, as I understand it. And recently there has been an attempt made, I believe, to make that stand up. And institutions that formerly did discriminate on the grounds of race or creed have had to change their practices.

PROFESSOR CUSHMAN: Yes.

MR. WILSON: I do know there are institutions in New York State that have had to right about face on the subject of discrimination. I happen to know one of them.

MR. TOBIAS: The proposed bill was to make that applicable to private institutions as well.

MR. WILSON: This has to do with any private institution or semi-private institution receiving State funds, and nearly all of them do receive a certain amount of State funds, as I understand it.

MR. TOBIAS: Tax exemption would be that in another form.

MR. WILSON: That is right, just another form of it, but somewhere along the line -- and I think we ought to find out about it in New York State -- teeth must have been put into that situation the last few years because there has been a considerable change. It may be a lever that we could use to the desired end.

MISS TILLY: Does the New York law take into account

CONFIDENTIAL

deductions of income for gifts to these institutions?

MR. WILSON: So far as I know, it does not. It is simply the receipt of State funds. If they receive State funds, at all [illegible] then they must not discriminate. I think within the last few years there has been considerable activity concerning that. I think we ought to find out more about it and what has caused the change, if any.

MR. TOBIAS: Part of it has been the threat of such legislation.

MR. WILSON: Probably. It might be a lesson for us.

PROFESSOR CUSHMAN: There was an action -- you probably noticed accounts of it in the press -- an action started against Columbia on that basis. They didn't succeed, apparently, in proving discrimination on Columbia University. What I gathered was at stake was the exemption of the Columbia University property from taxation.

MR. WILSON: I think in Columbia's case that was the threat. Have you any other questions for Professor Cushman?

If not, we will excuse you, sir, and thank you most heartily because I think you have been tremendously helpful to us and stimulating in your suggestions.

PROFESSOR CUSHMAN: Thank you very much for the opportunity. I enjoyed it a great deal.

CONFIDENTIAL

MR. WILSON: Ladies and gentlemen, this is Mr. Victor W. Rotnem, who was the former Chief of the Civil Rights Section, and is now a practicing attorney here in Washington. We are delighted to have your views on this subject, which we know is one close to your heart, sir, as it is to ours; and we would be glad to have you, if you will, give us the benefit of any statement that you care to make on the subject, and then we would like the privilege of asking you some question when you finish.

STATEMENT OF VICTOR W. ROTNEM,

FORMER CHIEF, CIVIL RIGHTS SECTION,

WASHINGTON, D. C.

MR. ROTNEM: I am quite impressed to find a group like this meeting on these problems. I know that you have, I am sure, hundreds of thousands of people interested in seeing to it that something real by way of a future program comes from your deliberations.

I have wondered much how I could be most helpful, having seen the work of the Section during the full war period. It is hard to make clear what we tried to do, unless we orient ourselves into the field of criminal law because we, of course, were a functioning unit, ~~more than a unit~~ of the Criminal Division.

The Criminal Division in Justice certainly has a large

CONFIDENTIAL

share of the toughest, dirtiest problems that come before the Government. After all, it is their job -- a group of specialists -- to fill the Federal prisons. When you came to look at the criminal law, as it affected civil rights, you, of course, found great differences of opinion among the United States Attorneys, ~~a vital part of the criminal field~~, as to what was and was not a good criminal case.

The appraisal of a criminal case, I am sure, is as difficult a job as any civil servants in government have to do. The judgments that must be made as to whether or not this is a case, whether or not these people merit the punishments that are provided in the criminal statutes, are very hard ~~matters of that kind~~ to make.

Now, I am sure you have had explained to you the history of why in the criminal field of civil rights there was almost from the beginning of the Section a control at the chief's desk as to investigations -- that is, the direction of them -- the direction of the case as it proceeded to the grand jury and from there to trial, looking at the process that goes on in relation to an estimate of a case, you have a bunch of mail, first, that comes in to you, or people come to see you with complaints. From that you must decide which matters merit FBI investigation.

CONFIDENTIAL

CONFIDENTIAL

Some of the best cases originally came on a penny card -- usually from the South -- but a penny card anonymous. Great mistakes were made and can easily be made in sometimes investigating a matter which didn't merit investigation. I am sure all of you have had some experience some way or other with the Federal Bureau of Investigation.

If you haven't, imagine yourself in a small town and agents come to investigate a problem such as a typical civil rights problem, or suppose you are the town banker and they are looking into some phase of your income tax. Does that investigation get around the town in a few days? It certainly does. The better investigations were always those where we had the benefit of not too much publicity, not too much fanfare, not too much overconcern about when we had started investigating; so that we might through the agents obtain those fundamental pieces of evidence that are required for conviction in a criminal case.

One of the greatest difficulties we had was that a civil rights case was usually so interesting, concerned so many people, that well-meaning folk would run stories in the press, would come to see us, run to the newspapers after they had seen us, petitioning us, urging us to investigate. Many a time it was wisdom to pretend that we were still considering investigation and to let it be known that we had started to investigate

CONFIDENTIAL

132

CONFIDENTIAL

about three weeks after we had begun, so that we might have that advantage of operation before souvenir hunters, and what not, were in the field poking around.

no ¶ Many times have best-meaning amateurs gone into a southern area meaning to help and actually hindered more than they knew. ~~It is all natural when you stop to mull it over, those ingredients at the beginning of a case.~~

One job that we never did satisfactorily do was to explain to the public the difference between the ordinary procedure of a grand jury in a State process as opposed to the preferable Federal system. The Federal grand jury, especially in our cases, was rarely a good vehicle for investigative purposes. How anyone could expect 24 ~~well-selected admittedly but~~ 24 average people sitting in a room to suddenly be learned in the art of investigation -- it just doesn't work that way. Accordingly, the best criminal cases -- certainly it was true of every one of ours that came to indictment and ~~conviction or~~ trial -- ~~that case was~~ were so thoroughly prepared by investigation before we went into the grand jury room that we could have tried ~~in the average situation~~ them the very next day. ~~Of course, the very next day was the best time to try that case also.~~

Any criminal case is best if, as we say, it doesn't get too old and have whiskers on it. Take the first lynching

CONFIDENTIAL

indictment in Mississippi during the war, which was a surprise to almost all of us. ~~The fact that a grand jury in Mississippi would indict under a lynching theory -- they did.~~ ~~But~~ That grand jury would never have indicted had they met the second day. They met, they heard this terrible story, they took a vote, and they voted the right way. Had they gone home and met again the next day, there would have been no indictment.

The only exception I know of where there was a long drawn out process was in Detroit in the Sojourner Case. There we did slave for weeks with the grand jury, and an indictment was returned finally. That was an exception. There was quite an affair during the war. I don't know if you all remember it, but it was in New Iberia, Louisiana, a terrible situation. A book was written about it later. Several prominent Negro professional men had to leave town overnight. I don't know whether any of them have dared come back even now.

It was so involved and we did deliberately try to supplement the FBI investigation with several days of grand jury. Maybe the result was good. The report they issued, or the stories that came out -- I am inclined to think, however, we would have done better had we used the process of Mississippi -- had we not been so much the sociologists as the criminal lawyers and pushed for that indictment, indicted, and put the defendant to

CONFIDENTIAL

trial. When you do that, I assure you you can't always be too fair. Any criminal prosecutor who has much success in the arts of getting indictments and getting convictions, I imagine as you look at him, talk to him, every once in a while you sort of conclude that part of the reason this man has success in his field is somewhere or other in his make-up there is a slight touch of the gutter. He can't be too concerned always, if he is looking for results.

I know that is very, very dangerous, and yet I am trying to give you that picture of the necessity of sometimes, if you want convictions, of using the artifices, using the things that, of course, well-trained criminal lawyers use just as the defense lawyers; and we have to admit when we get into this field that we are in the arena with one side bringing forth their best and the other side doing the same.

If you are going to use the criminal process in this field and if you want success, you have to bow to giving the criminal prosecutor a certain leeway. You can't hold him to too strict a standard, in other words.

Now, an interesting thing occurs when, as in civil rights cases, quite often you select a case because you see in it an excellent opportunity to test a question of law in the Supreme Court. Now, how is that done? In the criminal case if there

CONFIDENTIAL

CONFIDENTIAL

is an indictment and then the defense demurs, it is possible to have a direct appeal to the Supreme Court on a constitutional issue. It is one place where the Government, so to speak, gets a break in the process.

~~So in a few months you are in the Supreme Court on this issue of law.~~

The other way, of course, is that the defendant loses and appeals and it gets there as in Screws. Now, the average lawyer for the defendant is entirely too smart to demur and let us go to the Supreme Court because he knows that the chances are five to one ~~4 to 5~~ that if he will put us to trial, he will win an aquittal. ~~civil rights case in the South.~~ But I guess there are many lawyers, however, who are magnetized by the opportunity themselves to go to the Supreme Court on an issue. It was surprising how many of these cases did by this process go to the Supreme Court.

Then, however, you have a very interesting debate with yourself sometimes because in a civil rights case you may have the finest opportunity to get this test of law, as, for instance, in the Classic Case, which the Criminal Division had been working ~~on~~ for 20 years to have an opportunity to shoot at.

Now, the Classic Case was not a strong case. Really if you knew its facts, you would not be unreasonable if you were

CONFIDENTIAL

to say it was ridiculous to indict in that case; and yet by indicting, you had this issue, which went to the Supreme Court, and you had one of the great cases of the Twentieth Century.

So as the lawyer directing such a case -- and your superiors, who let you go with such a case -- you have to make that delicate judgment whether in spite of this being a weak case you are justified in going with it because of the importance of the question. That is a hard question to settle if you appreciate what a criminal indictment does to a man's record for the rest of his life. Poor Patrick Classic, I suppose, wherever he goes has this indictment staring him in the face and he will have to explain it between now and his death and after him, his children.

The other field where tests came in the Supreme Court, where the Section assisted, was in briefs amicus where in a civil case, usually a damage case, usually brought by one of the great groups, the Civil Liberties Union or NAACP -- in the final appeal, if the Solicitor General approved, the Government would file a brief and assist in the strategy of the case.

In that regard in the Department ~~it always has been this way and naturally always will be~~ the number of briefs amicus that go to court entirely depend on the policy of the Solicitor General. Mr. ~~Fay~~ Fahey was very helpful in my work when

CONFIDENTIAL

CONFIDENTIAL

I was in the Department. You could always talk to him about any case. However, he was not in favor of too many briefs of this type. His policy was very few. ~~Others would go to the other extreme and almost overdo it.~~ That, of course, the Section can't do much about. I think we petitioned for eight and received one while I was there. And yet I couldn't feel hurt about the negative decision of any one of them. There was a real difference of opinion.

For instance, one that I worked hardest to get was the Jehovah's Witness ~~[illegible]~~ Flag Salute Case. It wouldn't have made any difference if a brief had been in there or not. We thought so at the time, but when it was argued and all the briefs were in, I must admit they had covered every point ~~and~~ very well. But we would have liked to have felt we were in there doing something.

One other method ~~of course~~ that the Section could ~~such as that can~~ use, ~~although it runs largely to the bar, is~~ was the writing of law review articles on points of law that come up, ~~as they work on cases.~~ We did much of that, and that work is continuing.

I think to the lawyers in such a section there should be a constant encouragement toward such kind of work, that it should be as much of a feather in their hats as a conviction would be.

CONFIDENTIAL

CONFIDENTIAL

And also in the Political Science Quarterly some of the topics are, perhaps, better put there, and I think you have had a sample before me of one political scientist who was pretty darned interested in this field and pretty darned good, Professor Cushman. A whole lot of very effective educational work could be done by better informing the political science professors as to what the problems are in civil rights, including an understanding of what the problems are of men in Washington who try and do the practical work.

Convictions in civil rights cases in the South -- and practically every case was in the South, of course -- were had after we developed a group of southern trial lawyers. I never sat in a southern court room while any of our cases was being tried. If I had, as chief of that Section, it would have been a story and they would have been trying me. I would have hurt the case.

I did a few times sit back in the United States Attorney's office and try to keep my presence in the city quiet. I think the average prosecutor from Washington in a civil rights case is much wiser to conduct himself in that way unless he can become part of that community. Maynard Smith was one of the most effective trial men I ever saw in that field. He is not with the Section any more, but is practicing. He came from

CONFIDENTIAL

the adjoining county, almost, in the Screws case.

There you had the perfect trial lawyer. ~~You could bet that was a conviction, which it was on the first trial. Upon retrial it was lost. It was so old I don't see how anybody could have won it, that kind of a case, vicious as it was.~~ [redacted] The selection and training of a group of southern trial lawyers, who know how to work with United States Attorneys, has been essential in such a program.as this.

Almost always when the more important cases were developing the United States Attorney was invited to come to Washington, sometimes by our Section, sometimes by the Attorney General, sometimes by the Solicitor General, and he then received the background of why this case fitted into the whole program. His cooperation with the grand jury is so vitally important that if you do not take the time to let him know the background, you are apt to have no success at all.

I mentioned earlier the Sojourner Case. It was an exception where you had a length of time. The reason we obtained the indictment was, I believe, that the United States Attorney, [redacted] with the Washington men staying out of the room, [redacted] talked to that grand jury, man to man. He had lived with them.

You never bring these cases to the grand jury until the United States Attorney has had a chance to work with them in

40

CONFIDENTIAL

many cases. Sometimes the United States Attorney would say, "Don't bring this case to this grand jury. Wait until we get a new one." And about the middle of the next session he woull call and say, "All right, boys, let's go." That is the ABC's of this kind of stuff.

The whole Criminal Division, when you look at it as a whole, has in it many specialized groups. One group of men works on indictments, ~~who are experts at drafting them~~. There is the Appellate Section, which does the brief work. ~~That is largely in the Supreme Court and more so now in the Circuit Courts.~~ You have a group of trial men and a group of generally well-trained lawyers.

Now the Division is having its difficulties because of wartime cuts, but when we didn't have them, it was a pleasure often to be able to sit and actually make a selection from, perhaps, 50 men, as to who in Washington in the group were the best men to send on this case and find that almost always they were glad ~~tickled to get~~ to jump in and help, even though it wasn't in their field. ~~The interest of lawyers in government in~~ these cases ~~was so much more than you would think there was -- not the kind of men who go out and make a speech and join certain organizations, but as lawyers they were very interested.~~

So I point ~~that~~ out ~~to emphasize~~ that a great deal of help

CONFIDENTIAL

CONFIDENTIAL

comes to a section such as the Civil Rights Section from the other parts of the Criminal Division, and, of course, the Solicitor General's office~~, if there is an interest in the field, and the assistant to the Solicitor General~~ and the Attorney General's office itself.

A great number of these cases are of such importance nationally that the Attorney General just simply quite often has to take the file home and read up the facts and know it as intimately as the men down the line, and the Attorneys General do that. Every one I have known. And so with the Assistant Attorneys General.

Time after time, Tom Clark, as our boss in the Criminal Division, came in and took a file home Friday night and went over it. I do not know how he could cram the stuff in the way he did and come in on Monday morning and ask us the questions he was able to ask. He is an excellently equipped criminal trial lawyer. H~~e knew aht all the information meant and~~ pick~~ed it out.~~

Growing up in a division like that you had an informal method of trying a case in the office, trying it out just before we ~~was~~ were ready to go. Three of us would take one side and three of us would take another and we would bat it out and spend an afternoon. We might conclude at the end of it

CONFIDENTIAL

CONFIDENTIAL

that in spite of all these pressures that waive ~~[illegible]~~ a case to go ahead with. None of that can the public see or know of.

Now, moving over into the field of speech making, going about and making speeches and addresses to groups, I think a great deal more of that could be done than has been done. I think every ~~important meeting~~ in the United States ~~where there are over~~ two or three hundred attending, you ~~would want~~ them to ~~receive the proper information from whatever~~ group is primarily ~~charged with civil rights problems~~, whether it be ~~criminal or otherwise.~~

~~You get those matters in the Civil Rights Section because that is the only section people can come to.~~ Such speeches should be thoroughly prepared in advance. ~~You could talk extemporaneously,~~ but you should have it ~~before~~ you. A good part is the later distribution of those speeches. They should follow a program that you are developing so that at the end of a year you have a series of 18 or 20 addresses which almost merit publication. ~~There should be some careful thought.~~

I am sure you have all heard of the great amount of time that the Section spent with crack-pots. Sometimes they are totally crazy people who either write letters or come in person. And entirely too much time has to be spent on that problem by men who are so well equipped that they shouldn't be burdened

CONFIDENTIAL

with it, but God knows how else you could do it. Many times the Chief of the Section has to take on a couple of hours a day listening to one or two of them. In the case of some of them, if you called up the District Building and guided them over there, they would be at St. Elizabeth's by 6 o'clock.

Every group has that in the field. In regard to the Civil Liberties Union here, the local person handling it, the young lady is doing the job just for the fun of it. People come in and she sends them to me. It is the same type, pathetic stuff. You have to just take them and give them an hour and listen to them. You are sort of in prison. It would be nice if something could be done about that in the Department to save the time of these men and women who are wasting it there.

By the same token, you can't answer every piece of mail that comes to you because you have to become an expert in picking out the "nut" mail. If you answered everything, it would come and come and come. There are still people who continue to send in communications even though they are not answered.

And then, of course, you see the pressure groups and their methods, how they wire, write, and cut coupons and papers -- a ridiculous waste of money and effort.

CONFIDENTIAL

I am trying to jump to different things now, trying to think of things as they strike me now. Another phase of this work, in the viewpoint of government men, is the problem of the press and the pressure groups who are interested in specialized fields of civil rights.

Naturally, your labor union groups will be so interested if it is a civil rights case involving a labor union, but try and interest some tough labor leader in a problem involving Jehovah's Witnesses and he thinks you are a little off the beam.

Many men who have an interest in this field have just a hobby interest, a very sincere one, in one small segment of the field; and, of course, sometimes their hobby leads them into an enthusiasm which I guess the discipline of government has to calm down a bit. You couldn't go along with them as much as you might like to. Pressure groups are very often unfair on the men in the Section, by asking the impossible, ~~leaving~~ to many times. I suppose, when they ~~have a case, even though~~ a good ~~case, they have to, for their own existence, continue~~ to look ~~like they are the bunch that~~ is making this ~~immovable~~ object, the Government~~, get to work.~~

Many of the leaders of such groups could do much self-education and much study as to the possible areas where we may

CONFIDENTIAL

CONFIDENTIAL

operate as a civil rights group. They should know those limitations better than the men in the Government themselves.

On the other hand, the very groups that I am criticizing, however, in another way are the most helpful of all groups to the Section. They keep it on its toes. They bring the problems to it and assist in a hundred different way. Large groups always come in after some terrific episode such as a lynching or some special case that gets worked on like the boy's case down in Virginia where he was about to be hung the next morning. In those cases large groups come in.

Thurgood Marshall, General Counsel of the NAACP, would almost always be in such a group, and he would sit sometimes a couple of chairs away and would himself do the kind of work that I think leaders should do more of and tell his people what this was all about, bringing them down to earth as they would make these wild statements; and, of course, it was twenty times better that he tell them than that I tell them. That kind of responsibility groups should take. They should take it more. I suppose sometimes they are doing this disciplinary checking over of a case before they ever come to Washington. Of course, much of it is stopped that way. However, they have a responsibility to not bring in things which are frankly just junk cases.

CONFIDENTIAL

CONFIDENTIAL

I haven't any special group in mind when I say that. It is just that in the five years there were an awful lot of them. I ~~imagine there always will be, though.~~

MR. WILSON: Would you like to suggest or could you or will you suggest any special line of approach to this general subject from this vast experience that you had in the Section that you think we should apply ourselves to specifically, and particularly to be helpful to the Department of Justice?

MR. ROTNEM: It is difficult [redacted] to answer that without saying, of course, so much depends in the Department on who the Attorney General is. As long as you have a Tom Clark as Attorney General, you know that the criminal work involved in the Criminal Division, including the Civil Rights Section, gets every help it could have.

MR. WILSON: Except that we have been under the impression that there may be things that we could suggest -- procedures, changes, and so on -- things we could suggest that would uphold their hands a bit.

MR. ROTNEM: First of all, you have to appreciate that so much depends on the Attorney General and his policies in relation to this type of work, where you have these 96 United States Attorneys that, after all, are bound to follow the leadership of the Attorney General. They are responsible to

CONFIDENTIAL

CONFIDENTIAL

him, and if they know he is interested in one of these cases, generally they are interested in this case, even though otherwise they might tend not to be. I don't suppose there is any answer to an insurance that future Attorneys General have this interest in this subject, and yet it is your biggest difficulty always.

An Attorney General of the right sort will always see to it that this Section functions much as I have tried to give you a picture of it. You have probably had the picture so much that I bored you with what I said.

MR. WILSON: Are there any questions that you would like to ask Mr. Rotnem on the general subject?

MR. LUCKMAN: I would like to ask whether during the time you had this responsibility there was any occasion for prosecution of cases involving restrictive covenants.

MR. ROTNEM: Such cases were considered in the brief amicus stage a couple of times. I do not remember any set of facts where we could go with a criminal case or felt we could.

MR. LUCKMAN: There were no actual prosecutions?

MR. ROTNEM: No.

MR. LUCKMAN: Were there any investigations?

MR. ROTNEM: One, I believe, in Mississippi.

MR. LUCKMAN: Were there very many complaints received by

CONFIDENTIAL

CONFIDENTIAL

the Department in regard to restrictive convenants?

MR. ROTNEM: Not a great deal. It is interesting that there weren't more. It was not a field that people wrote letters about. The cases that were discussed as a rule were brought to us by counsel, who discussed them. Invariably on that question we couldn't come in with a brief.

RABBI GITTLESOHN: Mr. Rotnem, I would like to have your views, if I may, on a question we have already addressed to several people, but which you might, because you are an ex-chief of the Section, be able to voice an opinion more freely than they. Do you feel from the point of view of both prestige and possibilities of accomplishment anything would be gained if the Civil Rights Section were to become a division in its own right, rather than a section under the Criminal Division?

MR. ROTNEM: I have thought about this a great deal. I have heard it debated a hundred times, different ways. My conclusion, after my experience, is it would be a very bad thing to remove the criminal work from the Criminal Division. The judgments that need to be made -- as you remember, the Appellate Section, the men who handle the indictments, the other trial men, the Assistant Attorney General -- working with the other divisions, especially the assistance you get right in the criminal shop, you would never get that kind of

CONFIDENTIAL

CONFIDENTIAL

assistance if you had a separate division. That is the way government is. In this set-up the whole division feels like you are part of it, and you are.

It is one of the nicest government shops I ever was in, and I have been in many. They are exceptionally well trained men and nice to work with. I am afraid you would lose much more than you would gain.

Also I think this: If you set up a division or a bureau, you would have to go into a great number of fields beyond the criminal field. Maybe that is the reason you should do it, but if that does seem necessary, I would certainly say leave this criminal work right where it is, or you are going to do something basically ridiculous.

But what are the other things you would have this bureau do? Unless you have a lot more legislation than you have, if you set up a bureau apart from the criminal field, or have it with it, you will be creating a magnet for a vast number of complaints that you will have to answer, and without more legislation, all you will be doing is to encourage a vast correspondence unit, which will have to, in a thousand different ways, learn how to say "No, we are sorry, but we can't do anything about this."

I will be darned if I think it is good for our government

CONFIDENTIAL

j50

CONFIDENTIAL

to have to say no to citizens when they write to them, and to deliberately set up something where what will be asked

1-4 will require negative answers. When you set up any division such as this, you automatically spur groups to activity, to come and see you, to write you. Good -- if you are ready to give them something.

I would like to say something off the record, if I may.

(Discussion off the record.)

MR. ROTNEM: I think it would be fair to ask you what kind of additional duties you would think of if there were a bureau or division. Have you formulated some ideas on that?

MR. WILSON: I think the general difficulty, Mr. Rotnem, was as to just the question of if it was decentralized to that extent and there was the greater emphasis on it that might be brought about -- but I think and we have asked this question of a number who know the situation as you do, and the answer generally has been very much as you have given it to us, that we would really lose by such a move rather than gain in good results.

Are there any other questions that you want to put to Mr. Rotnem?

MISS WILLIAMS: I would like to comment, Mr. Wilson. Mr. Rotnem, isn't it true that the idea that came out of Interior as to a bureau was opposed by the NAACP not on the

CONFIDENTIAL

basis of the handling of criminal business but on the basis that they felt it would be an over-all administrative agency?

MR. ROTNEM: Yes.

MISS WILLIAMS: They were not opposing the handling of civil rights within a division of the Department of Justice?

MR. ROTNEM: No. It was somewhere along in the early days when they were starting to think of an FEPC. And this was almost another idea. It was about in there.

MISS WILLIAMS: There was a proposal that was dropped, and it was because it had that far administrative sweep and not the criminal.

MR. ROTNEM: But, of course, right away if you are going to have that division, you are going to have a tendency to put all civil rights work into that bureau, and the chairman of some Senate Committee might do that for you very nicely. You run all kinds of risks. Or the draftsman of some executive order may very nicely accomplish that, if there was no Committee like yourselves who knew what it was all about.

MR. WILSON: Are there any other phases of this you would like to discuss with Mr. Rotnem?

If there are none, I want to thank you very much for the time you have given us and your courtesy in coming before us and giving us this fine exposition of your own work there,

;2

CONFIDENTIAL

which is helpful to us. We appreciate it very much, sir.

(Whereupon, at 4:00 p. m., the Committee adjourned.)

President's Committee
on Civil Rights

April 11, 1947

Dear Mr. Carr:

Thank you for your kind letter of April 4, acknowledging my statement to your Committee on April 3 and commending the assistance which has been accorded you by this Department.

I greatly appreciate your generous words and assure you that it is a pleasure to cooperate with you in this important work. Please do not hesitate to call upon me whenever you feel that we can be helpful.

With best wishes,

Sincerely,

APR 11 1947

Attorney General

Mr. Robert K. Carr
The President's Committee
on Civil Rights
1712 G Street, N. W.
Room 309
Washington 25, D. C.

May 23, 1947.

The Honorable Tom C. Clark,
The Attorney General of the United States,
Washington, D. C.

Dear Mr. Attorney General:

As you know, the President's Committee on Civil Rights has been very much interested in the work of the Civil Rights Section and its attempts to provide federal protection against violations of civil rights. In its study of this program the Committee has heard, in addition to representatives of the Department of Justice, various spokesmen for private organizations. Many of these witnesses have been rather critical of the organization of the Civil Rights Section and of the procedures employed by it. The Committee has been impressed by some, of not all, of this testimony and it seems likely that the Committee will make certain recommendations to the President with respect both to the statutory authority possessed by the Department and the administrative aspects of its program in the civil rights field. Before it makes any decision with respect to such recommendations, the Committee would like to have the full benefit of the Department's experience and advice.

The following are some of the specific points which have been discussed by various witnesses and concerning which your advice is sought:

(1) Apart from the use of criminal sanctions is it not desirable that the Civil Rights Section be given the authority to employ civil remedies in situations where criminal sanctions are either unlikely to succeed or are ill-adapted to achieving adequate protection. Witnessed have touched upon the desirability of making increased use by the Government of civil suits for damages, for injunctive relief, for declaratory judgments. A further suggestion has been that the Department should intervene more frequently in suits between private parties by means of the brief amicus curiae.

(2) Many witnesses have suggested that the Civil Rights Section should be made a Division within the Department. Other witnesses have opposed this and I think the Committee is disinclined to approve any such recommendation. However, the Committee has been impressed by the statements that the Civil Rights Section can profitably use a larger staff or engage in additional activities. It has been suggested that the Committee should establish regional offices scattered throughout the country and employ field examiners or field investigators in order to provide on-the-scene examination of complaints, and also to provide a means of assistance and advice where no federal action is possible.

(3) In conjunction with the use of field representatives, the Committee is interested in whether the Section should be authorised to conduct investigation in advance of the receipt of complaints and to analyze situations where it is suspected that violations of civil rights exist. For example, it has been suggested that such steps might be undertaken with respect to the incarceration of persons in insane asylums and similar institutions where there may be a violation of individual rights.

(4) Interest has also been shown in the extent to which an enlarged Civil Rights Section might engage in continuous and comprehensive research on various legal and administrative problems in the civil rights area. The need for aggressive and imaginative prosecutions in the area, and the use of special prosecutors in criminal cases has been emphasized by certain witnesses and are of interest to the Committee. Some witnesses have suggested that the Section should keep a better statistical record of its activities and publish a more revealing and substantial annual report of its work.

These are some of the aspects of the federal enforcement problem with which the Committee is concerned. It would be very helpful to the Committee if the Department of Justice would submit to it a formal memorandum, stating its views on these aspects and providing technical advice as to how the organization and program of the Civil Rights Section can be expanded in an intelligent manner.

Members of the Committee have also expressed a desire that some of its staff representatives spend time in the offices of the Civil Rights Section acquiring first-hand knowledge of its operating methods, the nature of its records and similar matters. I assume that the Department would welcome such visits by staff members.

May I take this opportunity to thank you for the fine spirit of cooperation you have shown in working with the President's Committee and meeting its needs.

Respectfully yours,

Robert K. Carr.

July 9, 1947

Mr. Morris L. Ernst,
Nantucket,
Massachusetts.

Dear Morris:

Your "Notes Made on Way to Nantucket" have just come in and I am delighted to have you further reactions. I, too, thought the meeting went very well indeed. We are not entirely out of the woods yet, and I suppose we won't be until the finished report is finally submitted to the President. But things have gone a lot better than they might have and I am bullish about our prospects at the present moment. We are spending this week going over the transcript of the Hanover sessions and trying to get organized again. We will go to work on the draft report at once, but I doubt that we will have anything very much done on paper before August 1. I will certainly plan to keep in close touch with you and I hope you will continue to write to me from time to time as you have ideas.

I have not been in further communication with Mr. Wilson about the subcommittee to advise the writing of the report. As a matter of fact, I doubt that any such subcommittee will even function very vigorously. We will have to be in communication with various members of the Committee more or less continuously and as soon as we get anything very tangible down on paper it will be desirable to send the stuff out to all members of the Committee for their criticism as quickly as possible. So don't worry about that aspect of things. We will keep in close touch with each other in any case.

I certainly appreciate the yeoman service you did at Hanover. Your assistance was invaluable at many points along the way. You handled the discussion on disclosure particularly well and I must admit that it was a surprise to me that the Committee accepted the proposal so readily and so enthusiastically. Your presence and your remarks were certainly responsible for that result.

There is nothing I would rather do than make a trip to Nantucket this summer. My wife is particularly intrigued by the possibility. If there is any way of working it out you can be certain that we will take you up on your offer.

Yours,

Robert K. Carr.

CHARLES E. WILSON
570 LEXINGTON AVENUE
NEW YORK 22, N.Y.

July 14, 1947

Robert K. Carr, Executive Secretary
The President's Committee on Civil Rights
734 Fifteenth Street, N.W.
Washington 25, D. C.

Dear Bob:

Your good letter of July 11th, principally with reference to the date for our proposed September meeting, naturally raises a number of questions.

In the first place, I think, as I believe I stated when we were together, that setting a meeting as early as September 1st would be taking something of a risk and I am not sure but what it would place an undue burden on you and the staff. Postponing the meeting a couple weeks certainly would give more time for circulation of the body of the report and assimilation of it by the members of the Committee before our coming together. Frankly, I think this feature is well worth the delay, because I have no doubt we would get a great deal further, when the Committee meets, if the individuals have had time to digest the report, make their notes concerning any features with which they are in disagreement, or regard it necessary to suggest changes, etc. In these circumstances, I think we ought to have the meeting not later than the 15th of September.

Now as to the point of having only a two-day meeting, I have grave doubts of the ability of the Committee to do the job in such a short time. However, there are undoubtedly good arguments in favor setting up a two-day meeting, for if the Committee comes together with the definite idea that the job has to be cleaned up in that time, it may save a lot of pulling and hauling over non-essentials that would otherwise bother us.

Possibly the best thing to do is schedule a two-day meeting, with the understanding between you and me that if the "steam roller" does not work all right and we have to make some cumbersome detours, we shall insist on their staying a third day. What would you say to setting the meeting up for, say, Friday and Saturday, September 12th and 13th, with the understanding between us that if we really need the time we can go right through Sunday, the 14th? Certainly, if we encounter any snags that we cannot uproot in three days, we shall not accomplish any more by just adding to the days of the meeting.

I hope you had an enjoyable vacation and got a little much needed rest therefrom.

With best wishes

Sincerely,

CEW:H

---

734 Fifteenth St., N.W., Rm. 706

July 25, 1947

Mrs. M. E. Tilly,
1013 Highland View, N.E.,
Atlanta, Georgia.

Dear Mrs. Tilly:

Your long letter of July 18th has interested me greatly. There is no doubt that Georgia is passing through a veritable reign of terror and that shocking things are happening. Unfortunately, so far as any immediate action is concerned, we are entirely dependent upon the Department of Justice. The staff of the President's Committee has brought pressure on the Department with respect to a variety of matters and I think our influence is being felt. On the other hand, it is clear that the President's Committee is not an administrative agency and that, in the long run, its effect will be felt through its report. We are hard at work on the draft report and we are trying to make the sections on lynching, police brutalities and related matters just as strong as we possibly can.

I am keeping in touch with the Department of Justice about the Gilbert case. Fred Folsom of the Civil Rights Section has just reported to me that this case is being thoroughly investigated and that steps are being taken to get the Negro children out of jail at Hamilton.

Sincerely yours,

Robert K. Carr.

September 3, 1947

The Honorable Tom C. Clark
The Attorney General of the United States
U. S. Department of Justice
Washington, D. C.

Dear Mr. Clark:

I am sending you a copy of the report of the President's Committee on Civil Rights. While this report has been set in type, it is still in a tentative stage and I would very much like to learn your reaction to its contents.

The Committee is meeting in Washington on September 12 and 13, to go over the report and to endeavor to put it into final shape. It is our hope that it will then prove possible to have the final document ready for submission to the President around October 1.

It would be helpful if we could have your comments and reaction before the Committee meets on the 12th. It is, of course, clear that the Committee itself must make the final decisions on all controversial points but I am sure that the Committee will be interested in knowing your reaction to this present draft of the report, and I am sure that it will give very careful consideration to any suggestions you may desire to make.

If you would like to discuss any phases of the report with me or would like a fuller explanation of any of its provisions, I would be very happy to meet with you before September 12.

Sincerely yours,

Robert K. Carr

Enclosure

Woman's Society of Christian Service

Southeastern Jurisdiction
The Methodist Church

CHRISTIAN SOCIAL RELATIONS AND LOCAL CHURCH ACTIVITIES
MRS. M. E. TILLY, Secretary
1013 HIGHLAND VIEW, N. E.
ATLANTA, GA

Sept. 8, 1947

To - Mr. C. E. Wilson
Mr. Robt. Carr

This is a time of schools and conferences with me and I have just reached home to find the report awaiting me. I regret that I did not have it in time to write you earlier. I am deeply troubled about the report and will list first some of my minor questions and then will take up the parts that give me such concern. This all will have to be hurriedly done at it must be mailed at once to reach you before the 12th. I have no secretary and am not an expert with the typewriter.

In our table of contents under B . The Conditions of our Rights -
1, 2, and 3 are legal rights of any American citizen and are guaranteed by the Federal Constitution and most of the State Constitutions - but number 4 "Equality of Opportunity" is not yet a civil right, is it? Isn't number 4 one of the things we hope to gain through our report but something not yet realized. In the elaboaration of this number 4 , you make it a "must" - "must not only entitle.. must give him the right ... must be provided, etc". So, isn't it just of the "musts" we think Must BE. Should it be listed as one of the "condition of Our Rights".

As for number 5 under B, I am not at sure just what is meant.

I am afraid we are mixing the real with our aspirations.

I believe throughout the report, we are putting too much ~~emphasis~~ hope on legislation as a cure all. On page 5 under The Heritage and the Reality you use the words "quickly and effectively by the normal processes of democratic , constitutional government" It has not worked this way in the South and did the Volstead Act work?
Too much of the report is built on the premise that if we get legislation all will be well.

Now then, I will give you some more important objections -
I would most certainly not like to have you single out the Farmers Home Administration for attack. I knew the FSA well. I spent four months in Washington, at the call of the Federal Council of Churches , the Catholic Rural Life Conference and other organi - zations , working to save its appropriation. I rode with the FSA agents over many states. I know the great work it did for the disinherited farmer of every type of national origin in our country. Of course, I found it was not perfect, but I certainly do not want to single it out for attack. I have been busy this year and spent much Methodist money trying to save it from the economic scissors of the Republican Congress, so of course, I could not denounce it. If this comes out in the report as is, the Republican Congress might find it good cause to kill the whole agency .

Now about my South and the report.
The report is too beligerant. It is rather ficious as it raises a "whip-hand" against the South. It does not express an understanding of the problems of the South, but even drags in sentences to point up and at the sins of the section. I admit the accusations are just but we will have to use another method or else we undo the social progress the South has made in the last twenty-five years.

The report is too intol   nt. Aren't we attempting to te   tolerance in it, then surely we have just got to watch ourselves. The most intolerant people are those who are in tolerant of intolerance and this is what we are showing in the report.

The political implications of the report could be terrific. I doubt if Pres. Truman will feel it wise to sign it as it is. If he does and the report is really taken seriously (as we hope it will be), the South might speak at the National Convention.

I told you of my reaction to the segregation appraach at Dartmouth. I have been in summer schools and conferences week after week since then. We have had discussion on the "separate but equal" statutes of our Southern States . The question of one school system makes the groups always " see red". As I said before, the South will stay ignorant before it will be forced to having non- segregated schools. I believe every Southern newspaper will attack the report editorially on this score.

I am afraid, too, this will definitely kill the Federal Aid to Education Bill in Congress.

The sentence on page 20 at the end of the 2nd paragraph under the table is a maddening one. It certainly had better be left out.

I think the section on segregation will definitely kill any chance we might have of getting any legislation on any part of the report through Congress and will keep us from having a permanent Civil Rights Committee , the anger is going to be so great against the present committee.

Now for suggestions -
Omit some sentences so the report will be too much of a loaded gun against the South. Bring in some examples of the Northeast . There have been violations of civil rights there as well as in the South and West.

We cannot avoid facing the segregation question - but make it with a different approach. The report sounds like we are mad at somebody or some sections of our nation I think this whole section will have to be rewritten . It should not be so long. We must rewrite it , knowing that if we are not careful this section will so over-shadow the job outlined for us in number 2 of the Executive order it will seem that we had eased aside this burden and spent our time and energy on means of speeding equailty of opportunity and will end number 2 and all the rest of the report.

After all, do we not want to strengthen the civil rights of our people? Isn't this the real purpose of our committee? As the report is, it will be rejected by the South and the South knows how to <u>REBEL</u> . The school children of Chicago have this week shown they do also.

This, of necessity has been hastily written and I have said nothing about the fine points of the report and they are many. I have not expressed the thanks I really feel for the work of the staff.

I will see you on the 12th.

Sincerely yours,

Mrs. Tilly

Mrs. M. E. Tilly

I hope Dr. Frank Graham will be with us at our meeting.

THE PRESIDENT'S COMMITTEE ON CIVIL RIGHTS

734 Fifteenth Street NW., Room 706, Washington 25, D.C.

Telephone: Executive 3300, Extension 459

ROBERT K. CARR,
EXECUTIVE SECRETARY

CHARLES E. WILSON,
CHAIRMAN
JOHN S. DICKEY,
VICE CHAIRMAN
FRANKLIN D. ROOSEVELT, Jr.,
VICE CHAIRMAN
MRS. SADIE T. ALEXANDER
JAMES B. CAREY
MORRIS L. ERNST
RABBI ROLAND B. GITTELSOHN
FRANK P. GRAHAM
MOST REV. FRANCIS J. HAAS
CHARLES LUCKMAN
FRANCIS P. MATTHEWS
RT. REV. HENRY KNOX SHERRILL
BORIS SHISHKIN
MRS. M. E. TILLY
CHANNING H. TOBIAS

September 8, 1947

Mr. Robert K. Carr
Executive Secretary
The President's Committee on Civil Rights
734 Fifteenth Street, N. W. - Room 706
Washington 25, D. C.

My dear Mr. Carr:

First I wish to congratulate you and those associated with you for the splendid and exhaustive report which you have prepared, but nevertheless reduced to a minimum amount of reading matter.

Following your request, I have read the galley sheets, with the view of making possible constructive criticisms. However, I held in mind that the matter has not been proof read and therefore shall not comment upon what are obvious errors. I should, however, like to call to your attention the following matters:

1. Page 2 - "The Committee's first task was the definition of its assignment". I suggest the word interpretation rather than definition. In the same paragraph, page 2, "we must cure the disease as well as its symptoms". I do not think you cure symptoms but rather eradicate the same.

2. Page 6, paragraph 5 - "A minority, broadly defined is a group which is treated and which regards itself as a people apart". I am not a sociologist. This may be the proper definition of a minority. But as one who belongs to a

minority, may I state that I do not regard myself as a person apart, nor do I think that many other people of my race in America so regard themselves. Perhaps the majority look upon us as a people so far apart that the majority believe that we ourselves so feel, but I can testify that this is not true.

3. Page 7 - "the right of safety and security to the person". No where does this paragraph mention a fact which I recall Bishop Sherrill bringing out in one of the discussions, namely the right to life itself.

4. In proof reading, will you please notice that in many places throughout the manuscript such as page 8, paragraph 3, "the victims in these cases are not mutilitated nor burned". The sequence of neither or nor is frequently not followed throughout the manuscript.

5. Page 10, the last paragraph - "the Negro community which it feels owes no allegiance to legal order". I object to this unqualified statement and prefer that it should be stated that it owes no allegiance to unjustly administered legal order.

6. I should also like to call attention to the damage that the different standards of justice do to the majority. As a result of taking the law into their own hands, they believe themselves super men, depending neither upon God nor the law. While the minority must place their faith in a superior being, whom they believe will eventually level the scales of justice. Consequently the minority do not become an embittered people but strong in their faith, they are able to withstand mental as well as physical anguish. It is my honest opinion as a consequence of the treatment which the minority

has received in America the majority has developed a strong race of people composed of what we call minority races.

7. Page 11 - under the heading "the wartime evacuation of Japanese Americans", I should begin this sentence as follows:

"The most striking mass interference since slavery with the right to physical freedom", and eradicate the words, "We feel that we cannot pass without comment".

8. It is my opinion that something specific ~~should be added~~ concerning the number of Japanese Americans referred to on page 12 ~~and on the same page~~ I feel that the citation should be given on the California law, which forbids an ineligible alien to engage in commercial fishing. Similarly I think it would help the text if Supreme Court decisions were either referred to by name, as is frequently done, not always, or if the exact citations were given. not J-A

9. On page 13, you refer to the special problem of citizenship in Guam and America Samoa. Notwithstanding the fact that Congress is considering such legislation, I believe the Committee should recommend the same. is done in recs

10. Page 18, paragraph 7 - "The national organizations have been unable to prevent some local union". I suggest that the word unable be removed and the sentence read "have not prevent".

11. Page 20, last paragraph - "the argument loses some of its validity when applied to professional schools". I should have this sentence read "the argument loses some of its validity in ~~face of facts~~ and especially when applied ~~to~~ professional schools". no.

12. Page 24, paragraph 2 - I think should read,"it has been made clear to the Committee that unfortunately many public services, etc.".

13. Page 29, paragraph 5 - I suggest that the word "unwarranted" be removed from the first sentence. On page 29, last paragraph - "from my experience should read", "with practically no exception he is refused service". I know there are one or two restaurants which permit Negroes to enter, but also know that the complexion of one's skin has a great deal to do with whether or not he is served in these particular restaurants.

14. Page 33, paragraph 4, I should substitute "these private agencies have eased our burden". These private agencies have rendered invaluable service to the Committee.

15. I also suggest that the name of some of the prominent Protestant social action groups be quoted and the remainder covered with the words "numerous other Protestant social action groups."

16. Page 34, last paragraph - I suggest that the following words be stricken, "The committee believes...our land", and that we end this paragraph with the words "The committee believes that a single lynching is one too many."

17. Page 35 - I should like to call the attention of the staff to the use of the word national government in the place of federal government, which in my opinion is is the more acceptable term.

both are correct.

18. Page 36, paragraph 5 - "We believe this argument misses the point". I should remove this statement and substitute per-

Mr. Robert K. Carr
Page #5
September 8, 1947

haps "We believe that this argument is fallacious".

19. Page 36, paragraph 7- "This statement completely misses the truth". I should prefer "this statement overlooks the fact".

20. Page 37, paragraph 8 - "The court has not been niggardly or highly technical". This is another example of the use of or where nor would in my opinion be preferable. However, I object to the expression "the court has not been niggardly etc.". There are many people in America that feel that the Supreme Court ought to be highly technical. I should avoid any criticism from such personsby such a statement as "the court has with understanding underwritten etc.".

Page 37, paragraph 9 - "They should be encouraged to expect etc.", in my opinion should read "they should be advised that such a program etc.".

21. Page 41 - "Insufficient personnel" should be emphasized and enlarged by comparison with the personnel in other sections or divisions. ?

22. Page 43, paragraph 6 - in my opinion could be more forceful. Any agency that receives 22% of the incoming mail and to which the entire nation looks for the protection of its civil rights should have the dignity and the tools of ~~the~~ a division.

We don't want to make the rec. here

23. Page 45, first sentence of the last paragraph - "We do not have nearly enough" I suggest should read, "we do not have sufficient".

24. Page 47, THE MORAL REASON "It is essentially a collection of propositions about how people ought to behave". The American heritage in my opinion is much more than

above stated. It involves the responsibility of government to all the people and the concept of the exalted place of the individual. "All men are created equal". "All men are endowed with... inalienable rights".

Page 47, paragraph 7 - "It is impossible to decide who suffers the greatest moral damage". I differ entirely with this concept. Undoubtedly there are people who when denied their civil rights are weakened, but there also those of us who are strengthened by determination to win our civil rights. I refer you to paragraphs two and six of this communication. I often say that the minority are in America for the purpose of testing the moral fibre of the majority. We can, however, act in this capacity only if we are mentally, spiritually and physically prepared. Armed with this concept we are strengthened and not weakened by daily transgressions of our civil rights.

25. Page 52, paragraph 7 - in my opinion should be greatly strengthened. which ¶?

I hope the above suggestions will be helpful and that they are not too lengthy. I cannot close without again expressing my very deep satisfaction with the report produced by the staff under your skillful direction.

Very sincerely yours,

Sadie T. M. Alexander

STMA:afb

COPY

FEDERAL BUREAU OF INVESTIGATION
UNITED STATES DEPARTMENT OF JUSTICE
WASHINGTON, D. C.

September 9, 1947

Honorable Charles E. Wilson
Chairman, The President's Committee
On Civil Rights
Room 706, 734 15th Street, N. W.
Washington, D. C.

Dear Mr. Wilson:

I had occasion yesterday to briefly review a section of the proposed report of The President's Committee on Civil Rights in which there is criticism directed against the Federal Bureau pf Investigation in the way it has handled certain Civil Rights Cases.

I was extremely surprised to note this criticism because when I appeared before your Committee no member thereof questioned me as to the specific instances upon which the criticism of the Committee is based.

In your report you state that while the Federal Bureau of Investigation has performed some satisfactory work in the handling of these cases, in some of the cases the work of the FBI has not been up to the standards expected and that is followed by the statement that in one case an Agent of this Bureau, learning of an obvious violation of the Civil Rights Statute, failed to report the same to the United States Department of Justice, and in another case an Agent of this Bureau was accompanied by the law enforcement officer against whom charges had been made when the Agent proceeded to interview the alleged victim who had been abused by the law enforcement officer. In neither of these instances are any names given nor is there any way by which I might identify the cases cited and ascertain the complete facts.

As I have indicated, my surprise at the citation of these cases is due to the fact that when I was before your Committee I was not questioned concerning them so that I might identify the cases, make appropriate inquiry, and advise your Committee of the complete facts and take the proper disciplinary action which would be necessary if the facts are as cited in your proposed report.

I would certainly feel that before publicly criticizing a responsible agency of the Government that your Committee would ascertain the complete facts upon which such criticism is based, obtaining that information not only from the complainants but also from the agency charged, and then with the complete story and properly evaluating the same, appropriate comment might then be made.

I know from experience that there are many individuals, some well meaning but misinformed and others with more sinister purposes, who have made charges against the Federal Bureau of Investigation, which charges when thoroughly investigated have been found to be completely unsubstantiated. I think that there is no field in which more careful attention should be given to complete accuracy and truthfulness than in the field involving civil rights. I am particularly proud of the record which this Bureau has made in the investigation of the violations of laws in this field. I am not, of course, satisfied with the ultimate disposition of many of these cases by the courts and juries which have heard them, but that, as you can well appreciate, is beyond my control. Consequently, I am very much concerned that your Committee should propose to publicly criticize the actions and work of this Bureau without at least affording to me the opportunity of inquiring into those complaints which have been made against the Federal Bureau of Investigation upon which you propose to predicate your public criticism.

I do hope that your Committee will see fit, before finally approving this report, to supply me with the information which would be necessary to identify the cases which you have referred to in the report as indicative of improper handling by this Bureau in order that I may make immediate inquiry into the same so that I can supply you with such facts as I can ascertain and might be able to take the appropriate disciplinary action in the event the allegations originally made to your Committee are substantiated.

Sincerely yours,

(signed)

J. Edgar Hoover.

Vol #: 2
Number: 17
Ser.: Truman Pres. Library
Collection: Tom C. Clark Papers
Box: 66
File: Pres.Cmte-Civ.Rights-'47

President's Committee on Civil Rights

The Attorney General — September 12, 1947

Assistant Attorney General T. Vincent Quinn — TVQ:FGF:LAK
144-03-2

Tentative report -
President's Committee on Civil Rights

I have had the copy of the tentative draft of the President's Committee report checked over by the Civil Rights Section. It appears that we must be concerned primarily with the five pages numbered 39 KKJ through 43 KKJ, dealing specifically with the Civil Rights Section, the Federal Bureau of Investigation, and the United States Attorneys.

Mr. Smith and Mr. Folsom of the Civil Rights Section have checked files with the members of the President's Committee staff and have corrected a number of factual errors. In addition, Mr. Smith and Mr. Folsom have conferred at some length with Assistant Attorney General Ford and Assistant Directors Ladd and Nichols of the Bureau, and Dr. Carr. I believe from what has been reported to me that we could enter into an extended debate with the President's Committee staff over the accuracy of their conclusions with regard to the efforts of the FBI and the United States Attorneys. This would not be helpful either to the President's Committee or to us. I think we should instead take the position that we will welcome every criticism and suggestion that can be made by the President's Committee but that it will be a grave mistake for those criticisms to become public property. Within the Department we will run the danger of alienating the good relations we have had with our United States Attorneys without any compensating benefit. Outside the Department we will suffer a loss of prestige both from the standpoint of the persons whose rights we are seeking to protect and from the standpoint of persons who are prone to violate Federally-secured rights.

I respectfully submit that the Department's attitude must be that we do not wish to control the Committee's recommendations but that we feel those recommendations can be buttressed by generalized discussion. We should indicate that we feel the proposed discussion would have an immediate and possibly lasting bad effect on our efforts to enforce civil rights. We should indicate that we do not by any means desire that the President's Committee's study of the Department should be abortive, but we should suggest that if the Committee believes in the good faith of the officers of the Department their criticism of the two arms of the Department - the FBI and the United States Attorneys' Offices, can be made to you in a confidential report.

Probably these representations should be submitted by you personally or through Mr. Ford.

M. S' note to A.G.: Fred Folsom says Committee is making final report Monday. If A.G. has any suggestions, they would like them by that time. Is meeting again Sat & Sunday.

A G's note: I have talked with them & it's okey —

Original & attachments to Quinn 9-15-47

Vol #: 2
Number: 18
Ser.: Truman Pres. Library
Collection: Tom C. Clark Papers
Box: 66
File: Pres.Cmte-Civ.Rights-'47

President's Committee on
Civil Rights

November 5, 1947

Dear Friends:

I greatly appreciate your courtesy in furnishing me a bound copy of your report, imprinted with my name in gold lettering.

With kind regards,

Sincerely,

Attorney General

The President's Committee
on Civil Rights
734 - 15th Street, N.W., Room 706
Washington 25, D. C.

NATIONAL ASSOCIATION FOR THE ADVANCEMENT OF COLORED PEOPLE

20 WEST 40TH STREET, NEW YORK 18, N. Y.

LONGACRE 3-6890

Official Organ: The Crisis

WHITE

5th
November
1947

Dear Dave:

Madison Jones of our staff has just returned from a meeting called by Roger Baldwin at which were present representatives of five or six organizations to discuss means of implementation of the Report of the President's Committee on Civil Rights. This is the second or third such meeting which has been called. And there may be other organizations which have done the same thing.

We have called no such meeting as yet because we don't want to muddy the waters or to do anything which will prevent the most effective coordination. It is no criticism of the American Civil Liberties Union or any other organization to say that too often attempts are made to capitalize on enthusiasm without effective means of following through.

I sent the enclosed telegram last Saturday to Charles E. Wilson about a luncheon or dinner at the Waldorf-Astoria or a similar place, but have not as yet yeard from him. Upon hearing from him, it is our plan to invite a small but responsible group of organizations to join in sponsoring the luncheon and to work out a plan for a sustained campaign to implement the Committee's recommendations.

The organizations we have in mind are the following:

American Federation of Labor
American Bar Association
American Civil Liberties Union
American Jewish Committee
American Jewish Congress
American Legion
American Medical Association
American Veterans Committee
Americans United for World Organization
Anti-Defamation League of B'nai B'rith
Boys' Clubs of America
Boy Scouts of America
Catholic Interracial Council
Congress of Industrial Organizations
Council Against Intolerance in America
Council for Democracy
Federal Council of Churches of Christ in America
Freedom House
Girl Scouts
International Ladies' Garment Workers Union
Knights of Columbus
League of Women Shoppers
National Association of Manufacturers
National Association of Real Estate Boards
National Conference of Christians and Jews
National Council of Negro Women
National Education Association
National Federation of Women's Clubs
National Urban League
Union for Democratic Action
United Christian Youth Movement
United Parents Association
United States Chamber of Commerce
National Council YMCA
National Board YWCA

I am not sure that all of these would accept but we are going to invite them anyway.

At the conference today, Roger Baldwin mentioned that there was some talk of either the White House or the Attorney General calling a meeting of national organizations to discuss implementation of the report. Madison Jones didn't get clearly whether the White House had decided to do this or whether it was Roger Baldwin's idea to suggest to the White House that this be done.

So that you and we would not be working at cross purposes I tried to reach you by telephone today but the White House operator told me you would be gone until Monday. If you don't get this until Monday, I would be grateful if you would telephone me collect sometime before 3 PM when our Board meets so that I may be able to intelligently report to the Board.

I am still eager to hear the details of the two or three other startling projects you told me about over the telephone.

Ever sincerely

Walter White

Secretary

Mr. David Niles
The White House
Washington, D.C.

WW: emw

PERSONAL AND CONFIDENTIAL

Vol #: 2
Number: 20
Ser.: Truman Pres. Library
Collection: Clark M. Clifford Files
Box: 3
File: Civil Rights

THE WHITE HOUSE
WASHINGTON

December 9, 1947

MEMORANDUM -

Mr. Connelly called me at 4:30 p.m. and stated that the question had arisen as to whether or not the President should send a copy of the Civil Rights Report to the Congress. The President asks that I confer with the Attorney General on this subject and submit a recommendation to the President.

A copy of the Civil Rights Report should be obtained together with a copy of the press release that was given out at the time the report was published. After these have been studied, Tom Clark should be contacted.

C.M.C.

President's Committee
on Civil Rights

December 23, 1947

Dear Judge:

This will acknowledge your letter of December 19th, expressing your views on the Report of the President's Committee on Civil Rights.

I appreciate having the benefit of your suggestions regarding the proposed organizational set-up, and assure you we will be glad to give them careful consideration here.

With kind regards,

Sincerely,

Attorney General

Hon. J. Waties Waring
Judge
United States District Court
Charleston, South Carolina

November 12, 1948

Honorable Harry S. Truman,
President of the United States,
The White House,
Washington, D. C.

My dear Mr. President:

As one of the members of your Committee on Civil Rights, may I presume to extend my sincere congratulations upon your triumphant return to the exalted office of the Presidency.

It was my privilege to be chairman of the Nebraska delegation in the Philadelphia convention. I heard your address to the delegates after your nomination, and noted the power of your sincere and electrifying presentation of the issues to those present and to the great radio audience.

All of us watched with measureless admiration your unparalleled and inspiring direction of your campaign for election. Your untiring energy was unbelievable. Your courage and patriotism were sublime.

We of the Committee on Civil Rights rejoice in the vindication of your championship of our committee's report and recommendations. It is my hope and prayer that in your leadership of the nation and of the world in the next four years, you will realize the fulfillment of your exalted aspirations for your fellow citizens of America and for all mankind.

Sincerely,

FPM:PMcC

THE WHITE HOUSE
WASHINGTON

November 29, 1948

Dear Mr. Matthews:

It was with a great deal of interest and real gratitude that I read your very kind letter of November twelfth. Please know that such generous words of congratulations and commendation are highly appreciated. I shall, of course, continue to strive to bring about successful conclusions of the far-reaching issues before us.

Thank you for your helpfulness in writing to me as you did.

Very sincerely yours,

Harry Truman

We shall win that civil rights battle just as we won the election, I am sure.

Mr. Francis P. Matthews,
Insurance Building,
Omaha,
Nebraska.

White House Conference: "To Fulfill These Rights" (Johnson Administration)

EMORANDUM

Marvin Burns ←

THE WHITE HOUSE

WASHINGTON

10:20 p.m., Wednesday
April 27, 1966

FOR THE PRESIDENT

FROM Joe Califano

C

I have contacted the civil rights leaders about the 2:00 p.m. meeting tomorrow. Randolph, Wilkins, Height and McKissick will definitely be here. King is trying to rearrange his schedule and will call me later tonight or tomorrow. Lewis is in Europe but James Forman will be here in his place. (Nick and Louis Martin say they are about interchangeable.)

Whitney Young is in Nebraska and due to speak at Boeing tomorrow and at the Urban League in Seattle tomorrow night. He says he has tried, but cannot rearrange his schedule "without creating severe crises in racial problems" in Seattle. He asks that his Washington Bureau Chief, Mrs. Cenoria Johnson, be permitted to represent him. Do you approve this substitution? *

Yes ✓ No ______

Clarence M. Mitchell (Washington Director, NAACP, Civil Rights Leadership), Joe Rauh, David Brody (Washington Director, Anti-Defamation League) and Andy Biemiller will be here.

From the Government, we will have: Katzenbach, McPherson, Cliff Alexander and myself. In addition, Louis Martin will be there. (If you invite the press in at the end of the meeting, you should give Louis Martin time to leave.)

Do you want any or all of the following there?

The Vice President	Yes ✓	No ______
Bob Weaver	Yes ✓	No ______
Roger Wilkins	Yes ✓	No ______
Larry O'Brien	Yes ✓	No ______

*I have since talked to Young and we may be able to get him in tomorrow.

Nick recommends you invite Manny Celler and Phil Hart who will carry the bills in the House and Senate. Do you want them there?

Yes ✓________ No________

Nick is prepared to explain the Civil Rights Message and particularly the personal security portion which had to be redrafted as a result of the various Supreme Court opinions in the same cases.

I am attaching a copy of the final version of the Civil Rights Message which contains the changes you requested, as well as an updating of figures. I will have the signature copies in hand at the meeting.

Nick is prepared to brief the press after the meeting, speeches have been sent up to the Hill, etc.

Nick says it is likely that the Senate will be in session until 4:00 p.m. tomorrow, so the message can be received then. If not, Larry O'Brien says there is no problem in sending the message up tomorrow afternoon but letting the Congress receive it on Friday.

WHITE HOUSE CONFERENCE

"TO FULFILL THESE RIGHTS"

- - -

OPENING MEETING

WELCOME: A PHILIP RANDOLPH, HONORARY CHAIRMAN

INTRODUCTION: BEN W. HEINEMAN, CHAIRMAN

ADDRESS BY: THE HONORABLE HUBERT H. HUMPHREY,
THE VICE PRESIDENT

CONFERENCE PROCEDURES: EDWARD C. SYLVESTER, JR.,
VICE CHAIRMAN

- - -

9:00 a.m. to 10:15 a.m.

WEDNESDAY, June 1, 1966

SHERATON HALL

SHERATON-PARK HOTEL

P R O C E E D I N G S

MR. HEINEMAN: Ladies and gentlemen, good morning. I would like all of you to rise and join in the singing of the Star Spangled Banner.

(The National Anthem was rendered.)

Ladies and gentlemen, it gives me great pleasure to introduce to you the distinguished Chairmen of the various committees that have been established under the procedures of the Conference.

I would like them each to stand when I call their names.

The Honorable Edward T. Breathitt, Governor of Kentucky.

Dr. Kenneth B. Clark, City College of the City University of New York.

Mr. Jack T. Conway, Executive Director of the Industrial Union Department, AFL-CIO.

Mrs. Frankie Freeman, Commissioner, United States Commission on Civil Rights.

The Honorable Leon Higginbotham, Jr., Judge of the United States District Court of Philadelphia.

Mr. Theodore Keel, Attorney from New York City.

Mr. Chester Lewis, Attorney, Wichitaw, Kansas.

Mr. G. William Miller, President of Extron, Inc.

The Honorable James Nabrit, Deputy United States Representative to the United Nations.

Mr. Lewis A. Pollack, Dean of the Yale Law School.

Mr. M. Thompson Powers, Attorney, Washington, D. C.

Dr. Otis Singletary, Chancelor of the University of North Carolina.

Mr. Carl Stokes, State Senator, Ohio.

Mr. Percy Sutton, State Representative, New York.

Mr. John Wheeler, President, Mechanics and Farmers Bank, Durham, North Carolina.

I would also like to make an announcement in connection with a matter that has been of some concern to the invitees.

After considerable discussion, the council of this conference, which has been appointed by the President of the United States, and which consisted of a broad cross section of the interested groups in the United States, including, among others, the leaders of the six principal civil rights organizations, concluded that the taking of formal votes would not be in the best interests of this conference.

The reasons for this conclusion was that the report and recommendations to the conference consisted of broad, complex and numerous recommendations, and that, in addition, the conference was open to the suggestions, comments, or proposals of any member in connection with the report whether or not these proposals had been included in the report.

And that there was to be provided the freeest opportunity for suggestions and an exchange of views.

It was felt that in a two-day session, with 2400 participants, that to establish the conference on a parliamentary or legislative basis would be basically undemocratic in that it would deny to many persons who came here for the purpose of making their views known the next time an opportunity to do so because of the inevitable time that would be consumed in parliamentary maneuvers and discussion.

It was thought by the Council that a fair and desirable substitute would be a stenotype transcript made simultaneously and verbatim of everything that took place -- all suggestions, proposals that took place at the individual committee meetings, and that these would then be comprehended in the final report to be presented to the President of the United States.

There was, as I say, great concern expressed by all of the members of the Council, including those whom I have named, that to proceed otherwise would be to deprive persons not particularly versed in Roberts Rules of Order, not particularly skillful at rising in a controversial and competitive atmosphere, and would deprive such persons of the right to make their views known.

It has come to the Council's attention that there are present here a substantial number of invitees who feel that a resolution and voting process is a desirable and necessary part of a conference such as this, despite the views that I have expressed as being held by the Council.

Accordingly, last evening there was a special meeting of the Council, and at that meeting, in order to give the fullest effect to these views, the Council amended the Rules of Procedure as heretofore announced so as to provide that at the last sessions of the committees, tomorrow afternoon, the floor would be open at each of these committee sessions for such resolutions and votings as the members of the committee should deem appropriate. And again, there will of course be present stenotype reporters to make a verbatim and simultaneous transcript of what transpires, so that it may be included in the final report to the President of the United States.

I would now like to introduce to you one of the country's leading fighters for freedom, justice and equality -- Mr. A. Philip Randolph.

MR. RANDOLPH: Thank you, Mr. Heineman, distinguished leader of industry and Chairman of the Conference to fulfill these rights.

Distinguished members of the Council, builders of this Conference, the Honorable Hubert H. Humphrey, Vice President of the United States, I want to support the position presented by the Chairman with respect to the guidelines and procedures for the Government of this Conference.

Procedures and guidelines vary in conferences in direct relation to the realities that are confronted by the conference.

There is no set guideline for all conferenes, and in this instance, it was thought to be sound, as well as democratic, to proceed as indicated by the Chairman.

Each and every person in this conference will have the opportunity and the privilege to voice his views or her views in the last panel session, to suggest ideas that are not included in the report, and to present resolutions in the panel sessions.

Now, in the spirit of the conference, to fulfill these

rights, I welcome you. I welcome you to share in the enriching fellowship of the great and rewarding and creating experience, and the marvelous, wondrous, moral adventure, in a social enterprise to mark and achieve a new era of acceptance of the principle of the unity of the human family, and the dignity of the human personality -- irrespective of race or color, religion or national origin or ancestry.

Let me hail and salute the President of the United States whose vision and wisdom expressed in that historic speech at Howard University, June 1964, provided the inspiration and foundation for this conference, when the President stated in that speech, with boldness and humility, "But freedom is not enough. You do not wipe away the scars of centuries by saying 'Now, you are free to go where you want, do as you desire, and choose the leaders you please.' You do not take a person who for years has been hobbled with chains and liberate him, bring him up to the starting line of a race, and then say, 'You are free to compete with all others,' and still justly believe that you have been completely fair. Thus it is not enough just to open the gates of opportunity. Your citizens must have the ability to walk through those gates."

These declarations express a profound moral commitment to the highest ideals of the brotherhood of man. And here we are, men and women of the Church, labor, business, and government, assembled in a great conference, to become more deeply involved in what we more and more recognize to be the most tremendous social challenge of conflict and change in our country today -- the civil rights revolution.

It is our fervent plea for strong voices to be raised from all areas of our society, out of varying traditions and interests, to arouse the conscience of our land in order to achieve in fact that which has already been won in law, and what always has been in the hearts of good men -- equality, justice, freedom, and human dignity for all men regardless of color or country.

To millions of people of the Old World, America represented a land of promise, a land where people were free, a land where the individual could move about and up in his opportunities, his job, his income, and his social status. America was hope, it was promises. This meant horizontal and vertical mobility -- where a man could better himself, the level he could find was largely up to him.

It was this vision of a land of promise that drew men and women from the Old World. True, practically all these people lived in ghettoes. Some of them may still persist. But for most of them the nationality ghettoes were only way stations, thresholds inviting the newcomer to make his adjustment, and then move out into membership in the larger American community.

But the problem of the Negro is different. The ghettoes we are concerned about are neither voluntary or temporary. They are, for the most part, compulsory, and permanent. Precisely because the Negro is a substantial part of the total population, and because it presents the critical problem, an extreme challenge to American democracy; this conference, to fulfill these rights, seeks to awaken and cause all Americans to make a serious effort to understand and face up to their moral responsibilities.

Of all the groups who have settled in the United States and have become a part of this Nation, Negroes are one people who were brought here originally against their will. They were br brought here in chains. The slave trade was a profitable business. Much of the culture of New England, and the life of Southern aristocracy were based on it. The people were in slavery and exploited so mercilessly, even by the Founding Fathers of the Nation. Although slavery had existed in the ancient world, and down through the centuries in many parts of the world, the American institution of slavery was the worst. Slavery had no rights in American laws, moral codes or customs, husbands and wives became separated, and children could be taken from their parents. They were denied education and any hope for a better life.

The people had a civil war fought over their condition, a war which divided the Nation with a bloody and bitter conflict, kept the slaves landless, moneyless, friendless, hopeless, and hopeless. To their deprivation was added the loss of a construction revolution, the rise of the Confederate counter-revolution, which virtually nullified the Thirteenth Amendment of 1868, the Fifteenth Amendment of 1870, and the Civil Rights Act of 1875, a United States Supreme Court decision of 1883, and the decision of Plessey against Ferguson in 1896, which handed down the doctrine of separate but equal, which provided the foundation of racial segregation and discrimination in this country.

Thus, after over three hundred years of slavery, the mass of Negroe people were the victims of segregation and inequality for another hundred years. And to these human agonies of physical brutalization and mental humiliation which were suffered by no other group in the population, I must add, a mark of color. Other groups had moved out of the ghettoes -- the Irish, ,the Germans, the Jews, Polish, the Italians. They had moved ahead in education and employment. They enjoyed exposure to the stimuli of America's material and spiritual development. They could better themselves and become part of a mainstream of American civilization. If they suffered from the prejudices of of their neighbors, they still had a fighting chance of changing, of overcoming the barriers of discrimination. But for the Negro, discrimination and segregation and organized persecution and intimidation were a part of the conscious and determined plan to hold the Negro down.

During the First World War masses of Negroes fled from the Southern plantations and rural and urban areas to seek jobs and a new life in the North. They were forced to settle in restricted areas in the great cities of the North. Here again they ran into the same patterns of Jim Crow -- these patterns of housing and employment, deprivation and rejection were not written in laws -- but prejudice, custom, practice, made for the same thing. Indeed, many will testify that the Negro ghettoes in the cities are firetraps, mice, rats and vermin multiply due to lack of adequate sanitation. The increase of the Negro population through migration from the South and the increased birth rate result in extreme density of population and overcrowding. People were hemmed in, unable to move out or escape the slums -- even if they had the money to move, the rents they paid are higher than those paid by their white neighbors. They get less of housing for the dollars they pay for rent. Instead of paying a fourth of their income for rent, they often have to pay as much as a third, leaving them with less money out of low wages for food, clothing, medicine, education, and recreation.

Racial ghettoes suffer a double evil. They suffer from racial segregation, and also from poverty.

The people have no margin of security. There are no shelves with extra food for the next meal or the next day. There are no bank savings or insurance policies, for the starvation wages require a weekly supplement of welfare. There is nothing the people can show as security for loans in times of unemployment, family sickness, accidents, or other misfortunes.

There is no wonder that life expectancy is shorter than that in a white community. The incidence of disease and death due to tuberculosis and cancer is many times that of the white community. Child death in the first days of life, in the first months of life, and year of life. is over twice that for other parts of the city.

To the physical illnesses we have to note the ill effects of family life. The man of the family is supposed to be the protector and support of the family. But if he is denied education and employment, if he cannot play his role as a husband or a father, the family breaks down.

Thus men plagued with force idleness -- women have to carry the burden of providing the income, and at the same time caring for the children. Is it any wonder that alcohol and narcotics and gambling and various forms of antisocial action are found in the black ghettoes? And is it any wonder that children and youth are damaged emotionally and mentally? The destructive and devastating impact of the ghetto too is frightfully continuous and total.

There are families that have been on Welfare rolls for two, three, four generations. The result is a sense of hopelessness and helplessness and powerlessness. But despite the seemingly insurmountable obstacles, most of the men and women of the black ghettoes struggle to find work and maintain family life. And despite adverse conditions, most youth remain in school and strive to better their condition. They try to believe in the American promise, and they try to obey the law and look forward to participation in the political, economic and cultural life of the Nation. But the youth that are damaged are incalculable.

First are those who lose faith in their families, in themselves, and in the larger community. They reject themselves and develop a sense of self-hate and despair. They accept any evaluation of themselves. Those who suffer from self-rejection tend to withdraw from the community. They undergo an inner death. They lose an appetite for learning.

Some meet with mental illness, and seek escape in suicide. Second are those who react with bitterness and rage. They are ready to strike against others. The respect for life and law is destroyed. They fill the jails and houses of detention and the prisons. Their hatered is against authority, and especially the police, who they consider their enemy, and oppressor.

They hurt not only the white population, but also they strike against the life and property within the ghetto.

Third are those whose anger becomes a social force of mass proportions. This is the volcanic force which builds its explosive power to a pitch that it breaks out into race riots, and in violence, such as is symbolized by events in the summer of 1965 in Watts, a ghetto in the city of Los Angeles. It took only a trivila incident involving police ineptness to light the flames of racial violence.

Those who participated in the riot were chiefly youth. They set fire to 600 buildings, destroyed 200 completely. They broke store windows and looted the shops. 36 persons were killed, a thousand injured. 4,000 were arrested. Over 150 md2 million dollars worth of property was destroyed or damaged. It took the National Guard to restore order.

Let me warn this conference that the Negro ghettoes in every city throughout the nation are areas of tension and socio-racial dynamite, near the brink of similar racial explosions, of violence.

What can be done to right the wrongs of the Negro people of this country? What can be done to bring about social and racial justice and fultill the promises of American life for all our people, both the black working poor and the white working poor. Is there any hope we can solve a deep-rooted and complex problem which affects the life of every American and threatens the survival of this nation? How can we abolish the racial ghettoes?

Let us realize that children learn their prejudices. They are not born with them. They learn the ways of racial inequalities from their parents, from their attitudes and words and behavior patterns, and they learn from the experience of racial inequality, from the television, radio, press, church, school, playgrounds, employment, and government. Can we re-educate our children? Can we re-educate ourselves? Americans tend to believe in education as the cure-all for all ills. We must realize that the relations of the races and the roots of racism in the American culture are deep.

Because of these difficulties, it is unrealistic to

depend on appeals of the conscience and good will of the nation alone; because of the daily experience of segregation, it is unrealistic to think that education or racial equality and inter-group and inter-cultural programs can solve the problem.

If the Negro and the white Americans have to wait until their neighbors are educated out of their prejudices, they will be trapped in the ghettoes of America for generations to come.

If our people have to wait until everybody loves his neighbor, we may have to wait many a moon, or liberation will never come.

(Applause)

Most Negroes are not asking white people to love them or like them or understand them. They want their neighbors to accept them. They insist that they be granted the rights as citizens and human beings.

(Applause)

Thus the purpose of this conference is to involve all Americans in the great social enterprice of respect for the sacredness of the dignity of the personality of every human being which reflected in recognizing the rights of every person to life, liberty, and the pursuit of happiness. Every man's delay in breaking down the barriers of segregation in housing, schools and discrimination in jobs means irreparable damage to hundreds of thousands of human beings.

The damage is not merely to the Negro; it is a liability to white people as well. For we live in a world whose population is 80 per cent colored. It is no rational kindness to permit a white child to grow up in a home which is segregated, or in a school which is segregated, and in a white community which is an isolated sector in the total world community.

In the large cities where white people, white families have moved to the suburbs, the white child has been brought up without knowledge or understanding of his colored neighbor. A white youth rarely if ever meets or communicates with a Negro youth, though both are fellow citizens of this nation and fellow human beings.

How can persons or property be secured in a community where invixible racial walls keep children and youth and adults apart? Tension, fear and hate are likely to plaque persona lives in communities for generations unless we equalize conditions and plan for the transformation of urban life so that the great metropolitan comple-es are more truly democratic places of human habitation.

Finally, this is a difficult age, made so by the revolution of science, technology, and industrialism, and the revolution of the colored world for freedom and status, peace and plenty. Insecurity and conflict throughout the world d5

have made it an age of anxieties. Yet for each of us there are compensations. This is an exciting time, a time of change and new possibilities. If there is insecurity, anxiety, and fear, there is also a tremendous sense of possibilities beyond what men dared to hope for in the past.

This Conference to fulfill these rights will broaden horizon for the Negro and white American, and the entire world of color now in the revolutionary fames of discontent.

All honor to the President for his imagination and sense of innovation which made this conference possible. He will be remembered in history as the President of human rights, education, and anti-poverty.

(Applause)

And the civil rights revolution gave him inspiration and motivation.

The implementation of the report of the conference to fulfill these rights will constitute a major and powerful thrust giving Negroes the ability to walk through the gate of opportunity and achieve first class citizenship in America. Men and women, black and white, Catholic, Jew and Protestant, participating in this conference -- could ye like men be strong, we shall overcome.

(Applause)

Haoeun

MR. HEINEMAN: Thank you so very much, Mr. Randolph.

Ladies and gentlemen, the Vice President of the

(Applause)

STATEMENT OF HONORABLE HUBERT H. HUMPHREY,

VICE PRESIDENT OF THE UNITED STATES

VICE PRESIDENT HUMPHREY: Chairman Heineman, Members of the Council, our dear and respected friend, A. Phillip Randolf, whose hallmark of character is his great sense of integrity --

(Applause)

-- Philip, I feel as if I am privileged today to deliver a rather extended benediction to an inspiring invocation by you, sir.

The first lines of my remarks to this historic conference is -- we know why we are here, and indeed we have heard the call. And we have heard the call to action sounded by President Johnson at Howard University, a call challenging America to move from opportunity to achievement, to realize not just equality as a right and a theory, but equality as a fact, and equality as a result.

Now, we know the intensive work which hundreds of persons have expended in preparing for this conference -- the spirited deliberations of the planning session in November, the reports of task forces and panels, and the challenging report and recommendations prepared by the Counsel to this conference.

I trust that each and every one of us has studied that

report and the recommendations included therein carefully.

But we are here to go to work, and there is much work to be done. In a few short years we have traveled down a road studded with landmarks, historic court decisions, legislative victories, and executive actions. And as we have traveled that road, we have seen a thousand acts of heroism, large and small, by the brave and determined Americans who have made that journey with us, men and women of both races struggling to secure the reality of freedom, the reality of equality and human dignity. And of course we rejoice in these victories, as we rejoice in the knowledge that the troop of travelers, with a handful of courageous marchers a few years ago, has swelled to a mighty tide of humanity.

But our task at this conference, as it will be America's urgent domestic task for many years to come, is not to recount the progress of the past, but to fulfill the promise of the future.

Now, this will be a hard, sometimes unglamorous frequently frustrating responsibility. We can rejoice that the time has arrived when millions of Negro Americans can step out of the shadows and walk forthrightly into the bright sunshine of human rights. But a man too long walled off from society cannot easily adjust his senses and his capacities to the light -- yes, and the hate -- of equality.

This generation of Americans has the task, and I

md8 add, the priceless opportunity, of walking side by side with the Negro American as he strides into that bright sunshine and stands erect, equipped, trained for his opportunity.

Now, as we see the work before us, we cannot avoid the realization that many times our deeds have not matched our words, that there still exists a tragic gap separating promise from performance in the many crucial areas of civil rights policy.

What more explicit documentation of this do we need than was given to us this morning by A. Philip Randolph. And that performance gap that I have referred to must be closed.

(Applause)

The blame for that gap cannot be laid at the feet of any single person or institution. Every major segment of our society has contribted to maintaining this gap between promise and performance. So we ask the question -- how are we to close it?

Well, the first requirement is to concede that it exists -- unflinching, unblinking candor is an absolute necessity if we are to prevail, as prevail we must, in the new stage, this the new stage of the civil rights battle.

Now, as I see it here are the major areas where we must do much better.

First, the Federal Government has the job of

meeting its growing responsibilities. And I have no doubt that this topic will receive more than its share of attention in the next two days.

(Applause)

But permit me this observation -- as a member of the federal establishment. Despite the Federal Government's absolute commitment to achieving equality for all Americans, and its accomplishments of the past, and those which will be evident in the future, we welcome constructive evaluation and criticism of our efforts to implement all civil rights statutes and policies and to carry forward our struggle against deprivation and discrimination. And on behalf of President Johnson, I give you this pledge. The Federal Government will improve its performance wherever that is necessary. We will not shirk our responsibilities.

(Applause)

MILLS
rh fls
md

Secondly, states and localities -- states and local governments have often failed to exercise meaningful initiative in a wide spectrum of civil rights issues. Now, this deficiency is especially acute because it is in the state houses, the city halls and the town, local town meetings -- not just the halls of Congress or the federal courtrooms -- where the major battles of the next phase of the civil rights struggle will be waged.

It is in our states and local communities where we must gear ourself for action and wage war against what I prefer to call America's shame, slumism.

Let me describe for you this ugly term "slumism", related of course to the ghettoes that have been spoken of this morning, in our cities.

Slumism encompasses poverty, illiteracy, and disease. Slumism is discrimination and frustration and bitterness. Slumism is the ungathered garbage, if you please, and the dilapidated buildings. Slumism is a family of eight or ten in an unheated room. Slumism is danger on the stairs, and violence in the street. Slumism is rent so high that a desperate man is either moved to tears or to crime. Slumism is segregated, inferior schooling for those who so urgently need the best.

Slumism is inflicting upon our less fortunate citizens the burden of dependency and despair, rather than stimulating their capacity for self-support and self-respect.

Slumism is the pent-up anger of people living on the outside of affluence. Slumism is the decay of structure and the deterioration of the human spirit. Slumism is the other America -- the other America that so few of us seem to know, the America of the poor, the America of the deprived, of the unwanted.

But we can defeat slumism, and we can defeat it only if state and local leadership, working hand in hand with the federal government and the private groups, reasserts itself in bold and relentless fashion.

Thirdly, business and labor unions must move more effectively towards the goal of equal employment opportunity and achievement.

(Applause.)

I know, and I applaud, the progress which has been made in the past years. Of course there are countless stories of individual success which would have been impossible a decade ago. How well some of us realize this that have been in this battle so long. And I have seen the statistics, and the charts, which demonstrate the rate of progress for Negro Americans in certain job categories, and prove, at least to the man that draws the chart and recites the statistics, that everything is getting better.

But to the unemployed -- and often the unemployable -- man in Harlem or Woodlawn or Watts, these individual stories of success, and the encouraging statistics, are largely meaningless and sometimes insulting. When the statistical base, that base line, is sufficiently low, any improvement, any increase tends to look better than it actually is. The good news that a Negro has been appointed general counsel of a major corporation brings little hope into the life of a man who failed to complete fifth grade in a second-rate school.

(Applause.)

So in all candor, I will speak within my own criteria, the criteria that I ask you to apply to this conference. We must face honestly the mammoth employment problem which still exists for most Negroes.

(Applause.)

Outmoded training programs, tests, recruitment and personnel procedures, apprenticeship requirements, and promotion patterns often deny equal employment achievement as effectively as the old-fashioned "White only -- Negroes need not apply" sign that used to hang outside the factory gates.

(Applause.)

Now, your counsel introduced here this morning has recommended a number of steps dealing with economic security, job opportunity and welfare. And these proposals merit careful attention and detailed discussion in the next two days.

Finally, among the most potentially effective agents in our struggle to fulfill the rights of all Americans are our churches and our synagogues, service and professional organizations, and other community groups.

The heroism of James Reeb or a Jonathan Daniels has stirred the conscience and the soul of our America.

Many religious denominations and local congregations have given heartening evidence of their determination to infuse the concepts of brotherhood, yes, of love and justice, with real meaning and substance. As the floor leader of the Civil Rights Act of 1964, I can tell you that without the help of our churches without the help of our spiritual leaders, I doubt that we could have achieved victory.

(Applause.)

But let us say honestly what we also know to be true.

Some local churches still erect racial barriers at their doors, and many more do not speak out affirmatively on the urgent questions of racial justice which arise in our communities. Many service, professional and community organizations likewise remain silent in times of crisis. And the civil rights crisis is not political or even economic -- it is moral.

Dante said that the hottest places in hell are reserved for those who maintain -- those who in a period of moral crisis maintain their neutrality.

(Applause.)

I am sure that you will agree with me that in this struggle for equality, there can be no neutrality, nor can there be any so-called conscientious objectors.

(Applause.)

Now, imagine the cumulative impact of these organizations of which I have spoken, uniting in behalf of racial justice and equality. The report of your council describes Project Equality, a national program in which religious organizations use their hiring and purchasing power to promote equal employment opportunity. Consider the effect if every major religious denomination and local congregation actively participated in this program.

We have at our disposal vast reservoirs of untapped economic and social power to unleash against the accumulated discriminations and disabilities which afflict so many Negro Americans. This conference could make no finer contribution to the general welfare of America than mobilizing these resources without further delay.

We must, however, appreciate the difficulty of the remaining problems, and the dangers inherent in a period necessarily marked by frustration and disappointment. Events and trends of this period, my fellow Americans, will often strain the patience and the forebearance of many well-meaning people, black and white. The days ahead will be turbulent, and at times very frustrating. Indeed, we will require a depth of maturity and understanding seldom achieved on such controversial social and economic issues.

Today there are some Americans who see racial separation and exclusion as the remedy for racial injustice and the evils of the past. Now, segregation was a major factor in producing the hate and the injustices that we are seeking to overcome. Do we really believe that more segregation or more separation will still this hate and overcome this injustice?

I think not. No -- our entire American experience cries out against this approach, and our history books are fille with the failures of prior separatist movements.

One fact seems patently clear. The goal of freedom no will be attained precisely to the degree that we are successful in enlisting additional sources of strength in our march towards equality and justice.

(Applause.)

Then, too, today there are some Americans who wonder whether the struggle for civil rights will ever be over. They ask in a pleading voice, "What else can we possibly do -- after all the laws that we have passed?"

Well, we should have learned by now that laws and court decisions can only point the way, set the standards, they can establish criteria of right or wrong, and they can provide a basis for rooting out the evils of bigotry and racism. But the laws themselves cannot wipe away centuries of oppression and injustice. It is people, we the people, that must wipe out that oppression and injustice.

(Applause.)

We should have learned also that social revolutions

-- and that is what we have -- that social revolutions do not necessarily proceed on the basis of some predetermined comfortable timetable.

I am quite sure that George III thought our founding fathers quite unreasonable. I can imagine what he thought of Patrick Henry and Samuel Adams and John Hancock and a few others. I suppose he thought them even blatantly irresponsible as they pressed their demands to their necessary conclusion far beyond what the English must surely have felt were the bounds of good taste and the dictates of knowing one's place in life.

Well, today, my friends, there are Americans, many of them law enforcement officials, who quite properly see a danger to law and order in the flaring of anger and the release of tightly coiled tensions by the Americans who live in our squalid ghettoes. But these Americans would compound the danger by responding, not with even-handed justice to the few, but to the heavy-handed indiscriminate retaliation against the many. And today there are other Americans who see in the struggle for freedom and equality a license for irresponsibility and violence.

They are both wrong, tragically, explosively wrong. And they must realize they are wrong and realize it now, while there is still time to seek racial harmony and justice in America.

(Applause.)

There is, in short, an urgent need to build a new climate of mutual respect among all elements of society, for it is this absence of respect -- yes, Philip, this absence of acceptance of a fellow human being, and a sense of responsibility which lies at the roots of the hostility and the suspicion which today threatens the tranquility and the progress of some of our cities -- yes, of all America.

Today there are Americans, some of them on human rights commissions, who appear more concerned about preserving the status quo than rooting out the long-standing injustices to residents of their communities.

(Applause.)

I do not wish to be misunderstood at this point. Most human relations groups serve their communities with justice, wisdom and courage, facing issues honestly and seeking equitable solutions to complex and difficult matters. But in some cities the fact is that this is not the case, and where those instances are revealed and exist, they must be corrected now.

(Applause.)

And I can say with considerable regret that there are even some Negro Americans who appear more concerned about their own positions than about the plight of the less fortunate --

(Applause.)

-- about the plight of the less fortunate, less articulate members of their race. And I hold up as a standard for all Americans the man who spoke to us this morning, a Philip Randolph.

(Applause.)

Consciously or unconsciously, their interest seems not in securing the fruits of equality for their brothers, but, regrettably, preserving their own personel good fortune and accomplishments.

Now, to both groups -- and I can see that I am making very few friends with this candid evaluation -- but I am not here in a popularity contest.

(Applause.)

I am here as an act of conscience. To both groups the lesson of the revolution of rising expectations, which is not only in the foreign countries, but is here at home in America, must be writ large. That lesson -- 20 million Americans will no longer be pacified by slogans or tokens.

(Applause.)

They will not be satisfied. They shall not be moved nor should they be by such slogans or tokens. For freedom now is not a catch-word for a minority of Americans -- it is a moral imperative for all Americans.

(Applause.)

And we can strive towards it to the credit of each of us. We can defer it or distort it, or deceive those who seek it. But we do so at our peril.

We can achieve it only through specific deeds, hard,

visible evidence that performance is linked with promise, and fulfillment is an element of faith.

This conference, ladies and gentlemen, is America's opportunity to begin.

(Applause.)

Now, to some persons certain recommendation is found in the council's report which will appear to be radical, and outside traditional American procedures and practices. I am not unaccustomed to having that sort of thing said. But in evaluating these proposals, it is essential to pose this question to those who think the council may have gone too far. What are the alternatives? What are the alternatives?

My fellow Americans, if nothing is done to reduce the unemployment among Negroes, still about twice the rate for whites -- and what can we expect if the 20 percent unemployment rate for Negro youth is not reduced? What are the alternatives if we fail to eliminate segregated schools in both North and South, and bring into balance -- (Applause) -- and bring into balance the disparities in the equality of education. And you and I know there is a disparity, an intolerable one.

What are the alternatives if we are unable to banish housing discrimination and do not expand substantially the amount of decent, low-priced housing available to all? What is the alternative?

These are the questions which this conference and the

entire nation must raise as these crucial problems are discussed and then attacked. These are the alternatives which must be weighed. We must find the answers.

Now, I know I speak for President Johnson when I urge upon you absolute frankness and honesty in these deliberations. I can assure you that your words, your deliberations, will command the attention and the action of your government.

This government is not afraid to seek freedom now for all Americans.

(Appluase.)

But I trust that each of you will be searching for those areas of action which can be implemented by the states and the localities, by businesses and the labor unions, by private organizations and the churches and the synagogues and the people. For only as we mobilize all the resources and seek the commitment of all Americans can we achieve the momentum, the enduring persevering momentum necessary to banish discrimination and denial from this land.

So finally I urge you, as I have done so across this country time after time, I urge all Americans to view the civil rights movement not in the harsh glare, the distorted reflection of today's headlines, but rather in the more balanced perspective of history.

Do not allow your convictions to be uprooted, your steadfast course altered by the occasional excesses, the temporary aberrations, which history tells us must be experienced in any great movement towards social justice. History has a way of shrinking to proper size the episodes which capture the public's attention for a fleeting moment, and it has a way of raising to proper size acts of wisdom, of vision, and of courage.

Today, as few generations in our history, ours has such an opportunity, an opportunity to transform a great nation into a great society.

We ask no monuments, we ask only the judgment of history. Let the history books show that a great nation did not set its face against the tide of history, did not say "Thus far you shall come, but no further." Instead, let the history books show that this great nation of America said -- there is no more room in America for a them and an us.

(Applause.)

There is but one America, one citizenship, and one destiny for all. And then we shall crown our good with brotherhood from sea to shining sea.

Thank you.

(Applause.)

MR. HEINEMAN: Thank you very much.

Ladies and gentlemen, if you will now remain standing, and proceed to the committees to which you have been assigned by the number on your coupon book, we will now proceed with the direct participation in this conference.

This meeting is adjourned. May God speed your deliberations.

Thank you.

(Whereupon, at 10:30 a.m., the meeting was adjourned.)

WHITE HOUSE CONFERENCE

"TO FULFILL THESE RIGHTS"

June 1 - 2, 1966

Summary of Resolutions

Preliminary Note

In using this summary, certain matters should be noted:

I. In the interests of both time and space, the summary does not reproduce the exact language of the resolutions except in a few instances where such language is identified by quotation marks. In several Panels, the resolutions, in any event, were edited and often summarized by the Chairman or a resolutions committee. In other instances, it was necessary to deduce the sense of the resolution from what was essentially no more than a statement.

II. The "whereas" clauses or other statements preliminary to a resolution itself have not been summarized, and are only occasionally referred to where the preliminary statements sparked considerable discussion. In several Panels, the Chairman announced that in voting on a resolution the membership was not approving or endorsing the "whereas" clauses or other preliminary statements.

III. The name of the proponent of each resolution is given with full appreciation of its relatively minor value. Even when accurately spelled, it was often impossible to make identification because by the end of the conference people had stopped giving further explanations such as their home city to identify themselves. In many cases, the names are misspelled. Where no name appears, either the author of the resolution was unidentified, or as was very frequent, the resolutions were handed in to the Chairman or committee who reported them without identifying the author.

IV. The page numbers to the several transcripts indicate, for the most part, the page on which the vote or action was taken rather than the page on which the substance of the resolution appeared, although in a large number of cases, these are identical.

V. In the vast majority of cases, the resolutions were adopted without discussion, although in several instances, it is apparent from the transcript that a particular resolution reflects discussion by that Panel at an earlier session. In a few cases, I have indicated something of the character of a debate.

VI. In most cases, the resolutions were adopted unanimously or with no indication by the Chairman of any substantial dissent. In those few cases where the issue resulted in a substantial division of view within the Panel, I have added "majority vote".

VII. Resolutions which were defeated, as well as those which were approved are included and so noted. Resolutions which were submitted, but never presented to the Panel for a vote or an expression of its views are not included.

Charles A. Horsky

SUMMARY OF RESOLUTIONS

ECONOMIC SECURITY AND WELFARE

Many of the resolutions do not fall specifically under any of the nine chapters, and some which do I probably have failed to recognize. I have tried to do what grouping I can.

Introduction

Add to page 6, next to last paragraph, the thought that "a full employment economy is essential to all of this" [redacted].

Amend the preamble to include as a goal "economic security for all disadvantaged people" ([redacted]).

I

Metropolitan Job Councils

That such Councils be created only under Federal charter with adequate provision to ensure representation of Negroes and other minority groups in policy-making positions ([redacted]).

That such Councils be established only when they will not be duplicatory of existing agencies (S[redacted]).

II

Rural Workers

That Negroes be given preferential treatment in rural post office jobs *all other governmental agencies* (discussion rejected (1) a quota system in proportion to population, and (2) implication that qualifications for jobs be downgraded) (~~Lowe, V, 61~~). *preferential treatment (see I)*

That the Federal Government face up to the problem of rural farm workers and begin to provide basic and technical education to enable them to meet the challenge of automation. Also provide housing, *medical & nursing care.* ([redacted] 353). *& welfare services such as*

> (A similar resolution (Pelt, IX, 245). In Panel X, the preamble had a reference to U.S. burning of villages in Viet Nam, which proponent of resolution refused to remove, and the resolution was defeated (X, 20).

That the Federal Government supply poor farmers with trailer homes (Boynton, II, 70).

Create a rural jobs task force, and reorganize the Department of Agriculture arrangements in all States, especially the county agents (XII, 368).

Clarify paragraph 9, p. 15, to make clear that it does not suggest any encouragement of rural workers to migrate to urban areas (IV, 441).

That a program be undertaken in rural areas (1) to build one million new houses and repair 2.5 million dilapidated ones in the next 10 years; (2) desegregate Southern hospitals and build new rural ones; (3) rebuild 30,000 sewer and water systems; (4) build 50,000 new rural classrooms; (5) encourage self-help, low-cost housing; (6) on a crash basis begin to upgrade skills of Southern Negro professionals; and (7) make use of mobile units in all government services (Bennett (National Sharecroppers Fund) II, 64).

(A motion to do the same things in urban areas was also adopted. II, 65.)

IV

Government Financed Employment Programs

That the Federal Government assume not only the responsibility for training workers, but for creating jobs, with equal employment opportunities, in the public sector (this is a part of the resolution of "the Alabama delegation"; Boynton, II, 69).

That the Federal Government initiate for the unemployed a massive public works program under direct Federal management, and open State, county and municipal jobs for equal employment opportunities (stated to be directed to the Alabama situation; III, 322).

That a "TVA" be set up for economically deprived areas, to coordinate public works projects and human rehabilitation (IV, 442).

That a "CCC" be established in Watts for its restoration and rebuilding (Scott (from Watts), III, 338).

That the President immediately initiate WPA and CCC programs in depressed urban areas to relieve unemployment (Mills, II, 69).

That the President issue an Executive Order declaring a 1966 national job crisis, and fund work programs in Los Angeles, New York, Chicago and other areas where clearly required (IV, 453).

(Same in XI, 213)

Comprehensive Employment, Training and Counseling for Negro Youth

That the program of education and training for deprived youth be further extended, and a program be instituted to rehabilitate youth who get into trouble early (Mitchell, II, 76).

That financial incentives be provided to encourage wider participation in training of people by industry, labor and government (IV, 443).

That skilled workers be used in vocational training programs, rather than only certified teachers (IV, 443).

That a program like OIC in Philadelphia be adopted and promoted by the Federal Government, as it has Head Start, and OEO grants to cities be made contingent on the setting up of such a program (Hill, V, 58).

VI

Affirmative Actions to Provide Jobs

That penalties be provided which will in fact discourage discrimination in employment at all levels of government and by unions and industry (IV, 442).

That the Government must be effectively restrained from using economic sanctions against persons exercising their civil rights, and be vigilant in preventing use of similar sanctions by private organizations or individuals (IV, 444).

That the Federal Government negotiate with common carriers regarding their discriminatory practices, and if they don't stop invoke Title VII (Hardwicke, V, 63).

That the Federal Government establish a task force to recommend to the President methods and procedures by which more effectively to get Negroes into business ownership and management (Orr, IX, 293 (majority vote)).

That the Federal Government establish a task force to investigate the employment opportunities in Miami, Florida (this is related to Negroes having to compete with the flood of Cubans) (Young, IX, 280).

That the coverage of Title VII be extended to State and local government employees, and EEOC be given the power to issue cease and desist orders (XII, 357).

- That EEOC examine State FEPC enforcement procedures (XII, 358).

ADD OMITTED

That immediate attention be focused on the recruitment, training and employment of Negroes and other minority group members in HEW programs (XII, 359).

Add OMITTED

That both Government and private industry should be encouraged to employ persons with arrest records when the circumstances of the police record and the nature of the job suggest no real risk (XII, 371).

XVII 2.

VII

Institute Supportive Services

That a Department of Consumers be established, with Consumer Education and Assistance Officers in economically depressed areas (IV, 445) (some panels made similar proposals under "Education," which are summarized in that section).

VI .8

That day care centers be subsidized on a national basis by Federal and State funds, and legislation be enacted "covering maternity care and job security" (the mover indicates he wants the OEO program implemented on a national basis (Chisholm, V, 63).

XVI 1+2

(A similar resolution on day care centers, adding that funds should be available for construction as well as operation (Goff, VIII, 196).)

That the implementation of the employment provisions of the Council's report be put in the hands of EEOC, rather than the Department of Labor, and the EEOC budget be expanded accordingly (Barth, V, 51).

That a national clearing house of employment opportunities be established in the Department of Labor (explained as not inconsistent with, but a different way to express, Council's recommendation on federalization of employment services) (Powers, X, 153).

That special attention be given to the education, counseling and job opportunities for Negro women and girls (Fox, XI, 214).

That a structure be created to coordinate the work of HEW, Labor and OEO for manpower training (XII, 359).

That the non-discrimination regulations of the Bureau of Apprenticeship and Training be enforced (XII, 367).

That special attention be given to personnel and classification officers in the Federal Government, particularly HEW, to explore and correct the subtle means by which discriminatory practices operate (XII, 362). IX, 3

That USES be examined to rout out discrimination and violation of the Civil Rights Act of 1964 (XII, 370). 18

VIII

Income Maintenance and Labor Standards

That the pending minimum wage bill be enacted (Mrs. Jackson, I, 62B and again at 81).

(Other resolutions in support of strong minimum wage legislation (IV, 448).)

That on page 29, in VIII, 2, add:

"(d) establishing federal minimum standards for unemployment compensation programs concerning benefits, duration, coverage and disqualifications to provide an above-poverty income for workers who lose their jobs."

"(e) improving state workmen's compensation programs, including payments of attorney's fees, to make them a realistic means of providing a decent standard of living for workers who are injured." (Mayer, XI, 198.)

(Another resolution to establish Federal standards for unemployment compensation (IV, 448).)

That (1) household service workers must be covered by State minimum wage laws, (2) must receive social security benefits, and (3) training programs should be developed for such workers to upgrade skills and provide steady employment (Cowan, VIII, 195). (A substantially identical resolution, apparently sponsored by the National Council of Negro Women, was adopted V, 65; VII, 195; IX, 295, and XII, 374.)

That provisions be included in Chapter VIII dealing with the need to protect migrant workers, including portal-to-portal pay when traveling between farms, and pay during machine breakdown (Sutton, V, 73).

That Federal labor laws be amended to afford protection and encouragement of the rights of all workers to organize and bargain collectively (related to needs of agricultural workers; Feller, X, 156).

(A similar resolution in favor of extending labor legislation to farmers; Henry, VII, 353.)

That a program of guaranteed minimum income be established with the family the unit of service (XII, 356).

(Another resolution approved serious consideration of a minimum income allowance (Huse, XI, 302).)

IX

Welfare

That No. 5, p. 31 be amended to eliminate words "reduced or", in relation to residence requirements (IV, 445).

(Resolution favoring no residence requirements are: Balfour, IX, 291; XII, 355.)

That eligibility for welfare should be established by application and affidavit only (IV, 446).

(To the same effect, XII, 356.)

That nocturnal raids be penalized (IV, 446).

That rent ceilings, where appropriate, be established for slum housing, with reduction of rents proportionately as housing is substandard (IV, 447).

(A similar resolution was defeated in Panel XII, p. 349.)

That the Federal Government supervise the use of Federal funds to ensure the economic and political freedom of welfare recipients (Sawyer, X, 158).

That welfare services be made available to all children, and the failures of the known father to support the children should be no bar (XII, 351).

Other

That the report of the Council on Economic Security and Welfare be approved except as modified by other resolutions (IV, 450).

(The sense of this was implicit in all Panels.)

That OEO hire the people it is supposed to help and give them more and better training (IX, 292).

That bills by Congressman Hawkins and Farbstein now pending in the Public Works Committee be supported to make the Economic Development Act meaningfully operative for Negroes (Cawson, X, 157).

That the Federal Government should

(1) refuse new and cancel old contracts wherever discrimination against Negroes exists;

(2) expand the Fair Labor Standards Act to eliminate the discrimination now existing against Negroes and other working Americans;

(3) establish a $2.00 minimum wage now;

(4) extend National Labor Relations Act to every worker, including non-profit agencies and agricultural workers;

(5) repeal Section 14(b);

(6) spend $50 billion more in the next 10 years on needs of housing, health, education, community service and job training. (Willis (Negro American Labor Council), XI, 212.)

That birth control services should be available to all women, and the OEO policy changed (XII, 354).

That all legal barriers to interracial marriage, adoptions, foster home programs and all personal relations be eliminated (XII, 356).

That there should be built into every poverty program features to eliminate and penalize segregation and discrimination (XII, 357).

That private agencies contracting for Federal services should be required to sign non-discrimination in employment affidavits (XII, 362).

VIII 10 That the Federal Government should make every effort to remove political control from programs designed to help the poor, and Mayors and Governors should be excluded from chairmanships (XII, 374 (majority vote)).

EDUCATION

Resolutions are generally grouped under the three sections of the Council's report, with a number of general ones, and ones that do not otherwise classify, in an "Other" section at the end.

I

Equalizing Educational Investment

That the Federal Government establish a "triggering point" for the flow of funds to substandard schools, irrespective of the wishes of the local school authorities (Boynton, II, 70).

(Similar resolution, III, 325.)

That the Federal Government expend funds for education outside of the existing formal educational establishment (proponent urged that schools are doing a poor job, and funds should go to civil rights organizations) (Vivian, II, 80).

That school boards should provide flexibility in order to make equally available to all children the community's specialized programs (IV, 382).

That the Secretary of HEW should have discretion to reduce or waive matching grants in States which are financially unable to meet the requirements (IV, 382).

That the Federal Government, through HEW, assume responsibility for the quality of education in all parts of the United States (explained that in some areas it is deliberately poor) (Hicks, VII, 356). IV, 2.

Add ~~XIII 24~~ K2 ~~prepared funds~~ ~~F.~~ IV, 380

II

Reduction of Racial Concentration

That Title VI be amended to apply to desegration in public education of non-certified personnel (Jackson, I, 62B). III 1.

That Title VI be amended to apply to State, county and municipal governments (Routh, III, 350).

(Also resolution that the Federal Government cease using its funds on projects which result in discriminatory practices by State and local governments (James, VI, 87).)

?

These are general Title VI not only ED

That the Federal Government take steps forthwith to eradicate the almost total absence of Negroes in administration and policy-making positions in the educational machinery (Jackson, I, 66) (original language of resolution "with all deliberate speed" amended to "forthwith"). XVII

(Similar resolution IV, 403.) ?

II, 3. That the recommendation of the Council on page 40 regarding special efforts to integrate teachers be expanded to include "on a college and university level" (IV, 383). III, 3

That the Federal Government promote programs to correct the firing of Negro teachers on the grounds of race, and help discharged Negro teachers obtain employment (Bivens, IX, 278).

That Title VI be expanded to provide extensive in-service training for teachers and counselors (Noble, X, 160).

That the President instruct HEW to require strict compliance with Title VI, and use his own powers to the maximum extent possible to secure these rights (IV, 409).

(Several resolutions expressed concern that Title VI was not being adequately or strictly enforced; and, in some cases, that more funds were needed. I, 67, 77; III, 325; VII, 331; VIII, 198; IX, 251; X, 154; XII, 375.)

(The resolution was accompanied in several instances by long "Whereas" statements (see VII, 324-327, and IX, 249-251), setting out a picture of non-enforcement, etc. There was often considerable discussion of the "Whereas" clauses.)

(In one instance the resolution was amended to specify that funds should be withheld from any school that refuses to accept the HEW guidelines; VII, 331. In another instance, a resolution to withhold all funds from a city or State that refused to desegregate its programs was, after much discussion, withdrawn; III, 348.)

That the Department of Justice be urged to initiate a "crash program" to see that school districts comply with court desegregation orders, and use or get authority to direct schools to comply with HEW guidelines (I, 68).

(Several resolutions urged that compliance with HEW guidelines be required. II, 325; X, 134.) — IV, 403

(In connection with HEW guidelines, and in Panel II separately, resolutions opposed "freedom of choice." Boynton, II, 70; III, 325; VI, 93. One resolution requested their expansion to include de facto segregation. Fairfax, X, 134.)

That the Panel expresses its dissatisfaction with the pace, scope and significance of Federal efforts to integrate schools, especially the actions of HEW (Rosenman, VI, 93). II, 4

That the Federal Government fund some of the self-help programs like Operation Exodus in Boston (Calbell, VII, 319).

That HEW send down guidelines which will facilitate the changing of grade designations in community schools so that total integration would come into effect automatically and immediately (Higgins, VII, 320). II, 4

That $927,000 be restored to the HEW budget, that Congress give adequate appropriations and personnel to agencies with civil rights responsibilities, and that all departments initiate affirmative enforcement programs ~~under Title VI~~ (I, 77).

That the Federal Government support Sen. Edward Kennedy's amendment to provide funds for schools that wish to provide transportation to end segregation (McSorby, III, 305). — V, 3

— MORE

That Federal funds be available to local school districts through the States on general rather than specific conditions, so that faster and more effective integration can be achieved (Bivens, IX, 278).

That the Office of Education make the eradication of discrimination and segregation its No. 1 priority (Fairfax, X, 134).

That the President endorse integrated education as a national goal (Fairfax, X, 134).

That Congress should pass a law like that of Massachusetts relating to the imbalance of the educational structures and make Federal assistance contingent on integration of educational institutions (Drinan, XI, 227) (the summary of the proposed resolution by the Chairman, which is all that appears, was less than adequate).

III

Quality Education for All

That the Federal Government, in connection with State and local boards, set up seminars to give teachers orientation for teaching in ghetto or newly-integrated schools (Scott, III, 334).

That all teachers should take a course in human relations, including teaching and living in mixed and culturally deprived areas ~~(IV, 388)~~.

That all teachers be given psychiatric tests. Tabled (IV, 392).

That the Federal Government set up, in connection with State and local school boards, seminars to prepare teachers for special problems of ghetto and integrated schools. (A similar resolution asked expansion of Title VI to provide such in-service training.)

That there should be greater dissemination of information about existing programs (IV, 382).

That the Federal Government should provide funds to implement existing programs as rapidly as possible (IV, 382).

That National Student Defense loans should be continued on the same basis as originally conceived (explained as opposed to a recent amendment) (IV, 394).

That the Federal Government should reestablish the unused portion of G.I. education (IV, 410).

That the Federal Government should examine changes in the enrollments of private schools after integration of the public schools to determine whether it should continue any subsidies (Bickel, IV, 408).

That the Federal Government should make a more careful check on the use of educational funds allotted to local governments (discussion explained that funds were not always used for the purposes for which they were allotted) (IV, 403).

That a Department of Education be created (IV, 399; carried by a narrow margin)

That educational testing standards, especially those used for ability grouping, be examined to eliminate those which tended to favor certain parts of the community (IV, 405).

That the Federal Government give assistance to leisure education and recreation (IV, 413).

That Federal, State and local governments, and private employers, take affirmative action to develop new ways to bring the undereducated into professional positions (Quinn, VII, 324).

That HEW introduce programs of supplementary education to use child guidance, social, and health workers to enhance the learning skills of public school children (Williams, X, 159).

That the President and the Federal Government take steps to see that more Federal funds go to smaller colleges, especially Negro colleges, rather than to "the big 25" (Reddick, X, 159).

That a section be developed in the Council's report on consumer education, with special courses on buying food and furniture, and on conditional sales, with special emphasis on adult training (XII, 390).

That the Council's recommendations on education are endorsed, except as modified by other resolutions (IV, 411).

(This was implicit in other panels.)

HOUSING

Resolutions are attempted to be grouped under the appropriate chapter headings, with "Others" at the end.

I

Freedom of Choice

✓ That Title VI be strengthened by providing for administrative enforcement (I, 86). II 1. & 2? 3. add

Leadership Resolution?

✓ That the President and HUD exercise all their powers against discrimination by builders, renters and financial institutions where government funds or credit is involved (Norton, VII, 364). IV, 1.

✓ That the present Executive Order be amended to cover all housing now existing where a Federal mortgage guarantee is involved (I, 86). — III 1.,

> (A similar resolution at IV, 342, which makes it clear that the Panel also endorses Civil Rights Act of 1966.)

That the recommendation of "clear and affirmative guidelines" in No. 2 on page 60 is inadequate, and should be spelled out and made more specific (IV, 342). OMIT - Above Res

✓ That Fannie Mae should become a primary lender for Negro mortgage loan applicants (Partee, III, 306). — III, 3.

Identical II 34-35

That the President call a national conference of religious leaders to broaden support for "Project Equality" and the investment of church funds and the funds of individuals and nonprofit groups in integrated housing (Wilmore, III, 313, 339).

> (Other resolutions approved a call on businesses and individuals who believed in integrated housing to put some of their funds in it. Milgrim, V, 58; Ware, VI, 118; Scull, IX, 230.)

That the Panel endorse and encourage the community action programs recommended by the Council in paragraph e, page 62 (IV, 366).

That the Federal Government encourage the leadership of local communities to foster integrated communities, and insist that all workable programs include plans for this (Frey, V, 65).

That Congress be urged to enact a Fair Housing Act of 1966 (1) prohibiting discrimination in housing, (2) establishing an Equal Opportunity in Housing Commission, with power to initiate action on its own, and with $8 million in funds (Bishop, V, 46).

That the Federal Government continue to promote legislation to enable minority groups to move into all-white communities (Cervantes, VII, 364).

That the Federal Government bar as an urban developer anyone who discriminates in housing anywhere in that locality (Willie, II, 77).

II

Housing for Low and Moderate Income Families

That the Rent Supplement program be fully funded (I, 86).

(Same idea in Martin, VII, 365.)

That HUD and OEO fund the administrative costs of non-profit housing corporations using 221(d)(3) and make revolving funds available to such corporations (III, 319).

That 221(d)(3) be extended to widows and/or single persons in FHA mortgage insurance moderate income property erected by private concerns (Young, VIII, 193).

That a purchasing subsidy, in addition to a rent subsidy, should be made available (Young, IX, 281).

(After much discussion of the "Sullivan bill," which no one knew details of, and a $200 down-payment provision which is apparently in it, Panel IV approved a similar resolution; IV, 357.)

That there should be a program to lease housing for low and moderate income families (I, 86).

That paragraph 7 on page 66, dealing with rural housing, not be limited to migrant workers and older persons (IV, 359).

III

Suburban Communities and New Towns

That there be added to paragraph 1, page 68, "according to a timetable approved by the Federal Government" (IV, 359).

That ~~paragraph 6~~ No., page 69, read "be encouraged and enabled" (IV, 360).

That the recommendations of the Council's report on aid to suburban housing be conditioned on the provision of a wide spectrum of housing, including public housing (Warnke, VII, 371).

IV

Revitalizing and Integrating the Ghetto

That paragraph 3, page 70, be endorsed except that the Federal Highway Program should be specifically related to the relocation requirements (IV, 365).

That immediate steps be taken to stop concentration through high-rise public housing; that all public housing be in scattered sites; and that immediate steps be taken to reduce the concentration of Negroes in public housing projects (I, 82-86).

> (A similar resolution, suggesting assignments to public housing to reflect the racial proportion in the community (Young, VI, 100). Another would give an administrative agency power to bring action if necessary (Tucker, XI, 201, 202).)

That in Demonstration Cities, and elsewhere, there be provision for social services in public housing projects (Williams, I, 160).

V

Other

That the Federal Government enact legislation to guarantee:

(1) equal opportunity in purchasing a house;

(2) the same treatment for all in renting (except in two-family dwellings;

(3) equal treatment in securing mortgages;

(4) equal treatment for all while living in their homes;

(5) equal treatment from real estate agents;

(6) punishment for those who aid or incite to violations.

Also establish a National Commission with State, County and local units to enforce the federal housing laws (Morris, VII, 348).

That the Federal Government should insist on strict enforcement of health, housing and building codes before funds are made available to any community (Kline, IV, 370).

That no funds under Federal housing laws be made available to any community if discrimination is causing a housing shortage and unless it establishes an agency to keep an up-to-date inventory of all housing available (Powers, X, 33 (majority vote)).

Why not in Section I "Crowded Child"

II 5 & 1

IX

152–154 UNANIMOUS?

That a National Housing Conference be called (Brooks, III, 309). - not viable?

No Fed Conf ✓That the Federal Government [To] encourage industry wherever possible to provide integrated housing for its employees, and encourage Federal contractors to do so (XII, 345 (majority vote)). /The Federal Govt / X, 1.

✓That DOD through its Base Commanders make use of off-limits power to ensure that open housing is available (XII, 350). — XIX

That the Federal Government expend funds for housing "outside the existing formal housing establishments," and funds should go to existing civil rights groups (Vivian, II, 80). + er

Skip That the Council's report on housing be approved except as modified by the resolutions adopted (IV, 374; VIII, 171).

(This is implicit in the other panels.)

That the civil rights organizations be asked to stage a second "March on Washington" in support of open occupancy (Defeated) (Benedict, III, 345).

That the Federal Government address itself to local laws that are used to prevent residential integration, such as large-lot zoning (Defeated) (XII, 340).

ADMINISTRATION OF JUSTICE

Resolutions are grouped under Chapters, so far as possible, with "Others" at the end.

I

Protection of Negroes and Civil Rights Workers

That legislation be enacted authorizing and requiring FBI agents to arrest for violence against civil rights workers (Sobol, III, 311).

(Same, except resolution is that policy be changed to bring this about (IV, 152).)

That the panel is concerned at the failure of the Department of Justice to prosecute Southern local and State law officers who brutalize and harass citizens; that the force of Federal law officials be expanded; and that the President investigate the constitutional possibility of the existence of Federal police power (Mitchell, VI, 126).

That the FBI hire 100 Negroes (Hawkins, IX, 240).

That no person be allowed to serve as an FBI agent in his home State, and no assignment to any State shall be for more than three years (Miles, IX, 287; majority vote).

That J. Edgar Hoover be fired; that more Negroes be hired by the FBI, and that Congress investigate the number of Negro agents in the FBI and its enforcement policy regarding civil rights laws (Israel, IX, 236; majority vote). I, 6

(Two resolutions calling for Hoover's resignation were tabled by Panel XI, p. 232; majority vote, and a resolution to remove him lost in Panel XII, p. 387; majority vote.)

That the President ask for $2 billion to enforce civil rights laws (Hawkins, IX, 240). I 2,

That in suits for damages for denials of civil rights, counsel be provided at Government expense, cost to be paid by the defendant (XII, 386). I, 7.

(Similar resolution that lawyers for poverty clients in civil rights cases be paid by the Federal Government (Boynton, II, 70).) I, 11.

That the provisions of paragraph 1, page 83, should be changed to permit the victim, including an organization such as a church, to be compensated by the individuals responsible, or, if that is not possible, by the Federal Government (IV, 421).

That Section 1983, Title 43, should be amended to make a city liable for damages caused by its officers who deprive persons of rights protected by Section 1983 and any other rights protected by the Constitution (Lonescme, XI, 226). III

II

Equal Justice

That the President should appoint Negro judges and court officials in Southern Federal courts (I, 62C, 64).

That when, under Title II, there is a pattern of discrimination discovered, this should trigger Title I ~~([illegible])~~.

That when Negroes are defendants, proof that the prosecution has invariably exercised its peremptory challenges to strike Negroes should be enough to trigger application of the Administration's jury discrimination bill (IV, 430).

That item 2, page 90 should be broadened to include other types of legal assistance (IV, 432).

That jury duty should not be denied on grounds of sex, as well as race (Hymes, IX, 232).

(Similar resolution, XI, 236.)

That Section 201 of the 1966 Civil Rights Act be amended to read: "It shall be unlawful to make any distinction on account of race, color, sex, religion, national origin or economic status in the qualifications for service and in the selection of any person to serve on grand or petit juries in any state." (Rawalt, XI, 199).

That (1) lists from which jurors are drawn should be made available to all counsel well in advance of trial; (2) that the rights of counsel to examine jurors be substantially extended; and (3) that information on the race and sex of jurors be made available to counsel (XII, 385). V, 3845

That literacy tests for jurors be prohibited, except when judge rules it necessary in a particular case (Defeated) (XV, 424; majority vote).

That appointments of judges be conditional on psychological tests of their attitudes, etc. (Defeated) (James, VI, 88).

III

Police Community Relations

That (1) the Federal Government make available resources for the professionalization of police work; (2) that it see to the hiring and upgrading of Negroes and other minority groups* in the enforcement agencies under its jurisdiction; and (3) that it investigate whether membership by a policeman in racist groups is a violation of the civil rights of minority groups (CORE resolution, McKissick, I, 40). IV, 1.

(Identical resolutions approved III, 308; VI, 70; VII, 314; X, 167; XI, 199. In Panel VII, item (3) of resolution was withdrawn on objection that it implied guilt by association; VII, 221.)

* Added by Committee –?

That the President should call a conference of law enforcement officials and community leaders and take steps immediately to "soften the encounters between the people in crisis areas and the police" (Lomax, II, 46).

> (Same resolution V, 47; VIII, 184; X, 132.)

That the Federal Government call a conference of Chiefs of Police and other law enforcement officers to encourage a positive attitude toward the provisions of Title III (IV, 434).

That the President should encourage police departments to adopt positive programs of police-community relations, and discourage a "get tough" policy, including police dogs (Francois, II, 55).

> (Similar resolutions in favor of instituting programs in human relations for recruits and staff, IV, 433; and that Federal Government provide funds for workshops in human relations for police and community groups, Lamb, V, 66.)

That all civilian police review boards be established (Mitchell, VI, 124).

> (Same, with added provision that board have independent power of investigation. IV, 432.)

> (That there should be "grassroots" representation on all police boards. Nessin, V, 73.)

That there be an elimination of police practices and procedures which discriminate against the poor and the disadvantaged, such as stop and frisk, arrests for investigation, improper arrests for vagrancy and loitering, improper search and seizure, and inadequate representation by counsel (Pemberton, IV, 436; says it is intended to state agreement with Judge Bazelon and disagreement with the Attorney General).

(Similar but less detailed, Mitchell, VI, 124.)

That the duties of the police, including the FBI, should be expanded to include community services, and the military-type structure of police departments should be abolished (Miller, X, 165).

That the good offices of the Federal Government should be invoked to provide a study of the proper function of the police in contemporary United States (XII, 385).

That police training should be improved (XII, 385).

That there should be better police, with a decent salary (over $5,000) (Wessin, V, 73).

That the Federal Government seek to expunge the police records of first offenders who have "over a reasonable period of time" complied with the law (Wilson, II, 86).

IV

Other

That the Federal Government establish guidelines for the use of summons rather than arrest in the case of minor crimes and misdemeanors (Eskridge, V, 75).

That the use of the release of prisoners on their own recognizance be substantially extended (XII, 385).

That juveniles receive due process in substantially the same manner as adults (XII, 388; majority vote).

That the case of every prisoner now in jail be reviewed to see which are illegally confined, and all jails be integrated (Cox, II, 74-75).

That people in Mississippi be authorized to carry arms and to have them in their homes (Defeated) (Miles, IX, 290; majority vote).

That the Council's report on the Administration of Justice be approved, except as modified by other resolutions (IV, 417).

(Implicit in other panels.)

GENERAL

Many of these resolutions may be appropriately grouped under the previous four headings, but they appeared to me to be somewhat different. There is some attempt to group resolutions on similar matters.

That (1) the Conference supports the proposed Civil Rights Act of 1966, (2) opposes the cut of $927,000 from the HEW budget, and (3) urges the termination of grants to institutions that maintain a policy of discrimination (I, 91).

> (A mimeographed Leadership Conference resolution, of which the above is a brief summary (see full text at, e.g., VI, 63). It was also adopted II, 51; III, 305; IV, 458; V, 44; VI, 67; VII, 310; VIII, 175; IX, 247.)

That the President direct the planners of the Conference to redraft the report of the Council and set priorities, a timetable, a budget, etc. (II, 56).

> (This resolution was offered by CORE in several panels. It was approved in II, 56; III, 317; VII, 310 (with an explanation that it meant that civil rights had priority over the space program); VIII, 197. It was defeated in I, 54, and in V, 57. In Panel VI a substitute resolution was approved to ask the Council to develop a budget figure for its programs; VI, 78.)

That the President be strongly urged to use all of his powers to guarantee an end to discrimination (III, 327).

> (Same resolution approved at II, 38; VII, 312; X, 168.)

That the President emphasize the principle of the maximum feasible participation in Federal programs of the members of the community to be served (Johnson, VI, 79, 133).

> (Same resolution approved at VII, 310; VIII, 206; X, 168.)

That the President be requested to work with Governors, in cooperation with religious and private groups, to have State conferences to formulate specific plans "to fulfill these rights" ([redacted]3).

> (Similarly, a resolution favoring a similar conference in each of the 50 States and D.C. in autumn of 1966 (III, 318); that statewide, local and regional conferences "to fulfill these rights" be held using Council's report as basis, and sponsored by the Federal Government if State refused (Young, VII, 362); and that conferees try to set up similar local conferences, and involve business leaders (Bryant, X, 163).

Resolution by McKissick that United States withdraw from Viet Nam ruled out of order and voted down (II, 59-60) (also tabled I, 80) (voted out of order, overwhelmingly, VII, 317, and VIII, 202).

That President be urged to int ensify his efforts to bring Viet Nam war to an honorable end so that a greater level of Federal funds can be devoted to fulfilling these rights (Jaffe, II, 54).

> (Similarly, that U.S. make equal opportunity for minority citizens its No. 1 priority (McKissick, II, 60; Castle, VI, 98); that the space program be given a lower priority than the program to fulfill these rights (Stewart, II, 72); that the rise of defense expenditures must not be used to postpone, reduce or deny expenditures to fulfill these rights (IV, 449).)

That the report of the Council be endorsed, recognizing that its recommendations are neither precise, inflexible or exhaustive (Curtis, III, 316).

(Similar resolution Jackson, I, 56; Mail, VII, 293; IX, 226.)

That the United States Commission on Civil Rights organize a permanent National Conference on Civil Rights, to meet periodically in sections on specific problems and annually in general session, the secretariat to be supplied by the Civil Rights Commission (IV, 457).

That the U.S. Civil Rights Commission be made permanent (VI, 135).

That the Council be retained as an on-going body and that the President, in cooperation with the Council, call special conferences of selected groups to report what they will do to implement the Council's recommendations (McDermott, VIII, 192).

That the planning Council remain in session for one year to receive responses to recommendations (Lathey, IX, 274).

That another similar conference be called in one year and delegates to this one be deputized to implement its recommendations on the local level (Lewis, VI, 116).

That more women be added to the White House Council (Whickham, XI, 223).

That a further report on the Conference be mailed to all delegates (VI, 130).

That each conferee be mailed answers on what the Federal Government plans to do to eradicate its continued participation in discriminatory practices (Floyd, X, 164).

That the President appoint a post-Conference Committee to report in one year on progress in implementing the Council's report (Flippin, IX, 225; majority vote) (Berking, XI, 229).

That the Council's final report be more specific in defining which Federal agency has the responsibility for taking the initiative (Stewart, XI, 73).

That the President delegate to the Vice President the responsibility for coordinating and expediting Federal civil rights programs (Mitchell, VI, 128).

That the President should establish the necessary enforcement agencies to ensure that the conclusions of the Conference will be enforced on the Federal, State and local levels (Davis, VII, 350).

> (Similarly, that the best and most effective means for carrying out the Conference recommendations be pursued (Musgrave, VII, 369).

That the Conference seek goals of equal opportunity for all disadvantaged minorities (Young, VII, 294).

> (Similarly, that it express its concern over the limitation of the Conference to Negroes (Sharpe, VI, 120, 137).)

That the panel registers its disappointment at the conspicuous absence of representatives of big business in policy-making positions (Russell, X, 148; majority vote).

That programs for health and welfare for minority groups be strengthened, and the Federal Government intervene directly when necessary (James, VI, 85).

That Title VI be vigorously enforced as applied to health associations, and a national conference on health of Negroes and other minority groups be called (Holloman, X, 162).

(Similarly, that provision of greatly expanded health facilities get greater emphasis in the final report of the Council (XII, 382).)

That enforcement of Title VI with respect to discrimination on account of sex is as important as discrimination on account of race (Hymes, IX, 232).

That an all-out effort be made through all communication media to have acts of discrimination be viewed as criminal acts destructive of respect for law (XXI, 389).

(Similarly, that the Federal Government should espouse a vigorous program of public education toward a national policy of equality for all (Young, VII, 363).)

That each conferee dedicate himself to see (1) that violation of civil rights be promptly reported; (2) that their communities become concerned; (3) that local efforts are increased (McAlpin, II, 83, prefaced by statement that the goals of the conference are not only the responsibility of the Federal Government).

That because the Conference recommendations will involve tremendous manpower needs, a crash program to recruit and train such people be started (Vanden Bosche, VIII, 193).

That (1) poverty funds be channeled into areas of need even if local authorities object, (2) that jobs created be filled by the unemployed, train the trainable and channel more poverty funds into the lives of the poor, and (3) provide housing, job training and economic assistance to those forced off farms (III, 341).

That the Federal Government investigate the Seward Luggage Co. of Petersburg, Va., and, if it does not end its discriminatory practices, invoke Title VI (I, 73, 76; close vote).

That the Civil Service system be investigated, because incapable people can't be fired (Stewart, II, 73).

That the President appoint a commission to oversee all programs in Mississippi, and give it power to act in cases of discrimination (Dunn, VI, 132).

That the Federal Government should make an effort to involve the total metropolitan community in obtaining equality of opportunity in jobs, housing, education, civil rights, etc. (Cervantes, VII, 363).

That the Federal Government enforce its own laws, and believe in them (Israel, IX, 233).

That the Administration and Congress fortify the rights of direct and concerted community action on the part of victims of social injustice (Wingate, IX, 248).

That civil rights agencies be investigated to see how many Negroes are employed in policy-making positions (McVey, IX, 294).

EXTRA RESOLUTIONS

That Home Rule be granted the District of Columbia (I, 58).

> (Also, II, 37; III, 302; IV, 451; V, 76; VI, 96; VII, 311; VIII, 179; IX, 232; X, 151 (representatives of 13 national organizations expressed their support; XI, 225.)

That the Senate should ratify the Genocide Convention and the 1968 Convention on all forms of Racial Discrimination (IV, 438).

> (Same on Genocide Convention, V, 72.)

That a U.S. Museum of Negro History be established (Garrett, V, 66).

That Negro art be given emphasis in cultural programs (Alston, X, 77).

That the Conference express its outrage that the American Medical Association suggests that Medicare patients may be treated on separate days and in separate offices, and that legislation be enacted to prohibit this discrimination on account of economic circumstances (Horton, IX, 273).

THURSDAY BANQUET SESSION

June 2, 1966

The Banquet Session of the White House Conference on Civil Rights convened at nine-sixteen o'clock in the Sheraton Hall of the Sheraton-Park Hotel, Mr. Ben W. Heineman, Chairman of the Council, presiding.

CHAIRMAN HEINEMAN: Ladies and Gentlemen, it is now my privilege to present to you our distinguished and honored guests at the head table.

Starting at my far right--and I will again, if I may, ask that you may a genuine effort to restrain your applause until the conclusion of the introductions.

Starting at my far right, it is my pleasure to introduce Mr. Floyd McKissick, National Director of CORE.

The Reverend Walter Fauntroy, Vice Chairman of this Conference.

Mr. Burke Marshall, General Counsel for International Business Machines.

Mr. Clarence Mitchell, Legislative Director of the NAACP. [Applause]

Mr. John Gleason, Vice President, First National Bank of Chicago. [Applause]

Mr. Jack Conway, Director of the Industrial

Union Department of the AFL-CIO. [Applause]

Mr. Cleveland Robinson, President of the Negro American Labor Council.

Mr. Chester Lewis, Attorney, Wichita, Kansas.

Mr. John Wheeler, President of Mechanics and Farmers Bank of Durham, North Carolina.

Mr. G. William Miller, President of Textron, Incorporated.

You have already met the distinguished Bishop George Baber.

Miss Dorothy Height, President of the National Council of Negro Women. [Applause]

And, the most distinguished Honorary Chairman, of this Conference, Mr. A. Philip Randolph.

[Applause]

On my far left, Mr. N. Thompson Powers, Attorney, Washington, D.C.

Mr. Percy Sutton, State Representative of New York.

Mr. Kenneth Clark, City College of New York.

[Applause]

Mr. Andrew Biemiller, Legislative Representative of the AFL-CIO.

Mr. Vernon Jordan, Director, Voter Education Project of the Southern Regional Council. [Applause]

Mr. Donald Slaiman, Director of Civil Rights Department, AFL-CIO. [Applause]

Mr. Carl Stokes, State Representative.

[Applause]

I will pass the next gentleman and will present to you Mrs. Frankie Freeman, Commissioner of Civil Rights Commission.

The Honorable Ambassador James Nabrit,Deputy United States Representative to the United Nations.

[Applause]

Mr. Walter Ruether, President of UAW.

[Applause]

The Honorable Leon Higgenbottom, Judge of the United States District Court. [Applause]

And, it now gives me great pleasure, indeed, to present to you the distinguished Executive Director of the NAACP, Mr. Roy Wilkins.

[Whereupon the entire assemblage accorded the guest speaker, Mr. Roy Wilkins, a standing ovation.]

MR. ROY WILKINS [Executive Director, NAACP]:

Mr. Chairman, Distinguished Members of the Council, Guests on the Dais, and all the Distinguished Invitees who have participated in this Conference:

I wish to say that I regard it as a privilege and a great honor to say this word at the concluding meeting of our sessions here in Washington.

This Conference which we are concluding tonight, is properly but an expression of the revolution of rising expectations which has been in being among Negro citizens and their allies since the date of the Second Emancipation, May 17, 1954.

On that date, the legal blessing which had been bestowed for 58 years upon the doctrine of separate-but-equal constitutional citizenship was withdrawn in the historic Brown decision of the United States Supreme Court.

These past two days have brought the first-in-history White House Conference "To Fulfill These Rights".

There have been White House Conferences on health, children, foreign policy, education and other issues vital to our national welfare. Now, for the first time, the issue which has plagued both the national policy and the American conscience from Jamestown in 1619 to Watts in 1965, has moved to the center of the national stage.

Through most of our history it has been a matter for the states and for private organizations. We have cried out our anguish, voiced our protests and worked feverishly in patchwork efforts within the states, but we lacked the national recognition, of, and attention to, what we knew to be a national concern.

The handicap of the state perspective has been underscored no more effectively than by the correspondence in 1809 of Thomas Jefferson.

He wrote then to a friend:

"My doubts", he said, that is to the inherent abilities of Negroes, "were the result of personal observation in the limited sphere of my own state, where the opportunities..."--this is certainly the understatement of the century! [Laughter] "...for the development of their genius were not favorable and those of exercising it still less so, but whatever be their degree of talent, it is no measure of their rights".

The present civil rights struggle is essentially an effort by the Negro American minority, handicapped above other minorities by skin color and a slave background, to find, in Jefferson's words, "favorable opportunities for the development and exercise of their genius".

Our conference today called with uncommon courage by our President, has substituted for Jefferson's personal observation a White Paper of formidable facts, of fearless analysis and arraignment and of bold chartings of action reaching to the heart of the democratic ideal.

Since a survey of the vast variety of disabilities stemming from racial exploitation would require a month long conference and several volumes of reports and recommendations, four critical areas of living and citizenship were selected. No mere history of hardship, this, but a frank 1966 look at the present and into the future.

For example, on the section on Economic Security and Welfare, this sentence: "No more ugly and urgent crisis facing this nation today that the economic insecurity of Negro Americans. Employment and income problems are complex, long standing and rooted deeply. Negro unemployment is of disaster proportions. Creative and large scale action must be taken to achieve full and fair employment for the Negro working age population".

And, this from the section on Education:

"American schools today are failing to fulfill their purpose of preparing children to be independent persons in an open society. It is incontestable that we have different qualities of education and therefore widely varying levels of opportunity through schooling for the Negro child and the white child. More than 90 per cent of school children are educated in racially segregated schools which provide inferior education through their failure..." and I quote as direct "...to prepare their pupils for life in our pluralistic society and ever-shrinking world; defacto segregation continues as the prevailing pattern in the north and west, and if anything, has become more, rather than less, rigid".

On housing, "The consequences of the slums and the ghettoes and the barriers to freedom of choice in housing loom large. The dimensions of this program that is, of massive building and rehabilitation programs, are staggering but they are no larger than American's space ventures".

The rent supplement and Demonstration City we urgently recommend.

On administration of justice three categories were set forth embracing protection of Negroes and civil rights workers in connection with the exercise of their rights. Equal justice in the operation of the machinery of the law, that is juries, courts, court officials and law enforcement agents and police minority group community relations.

The material in the Council report, including the recommendations for action, has received critical scrutiny and has benefited from broadening and strengthening corrections and amendments, including home rule for D.C. [Applause] --by the conferees in the twelve committees.

Each of these urgent suggestions--and obviously, there isn't time here to list all of them. One of the participants came to me triumphantly and said, "You know, we passed fifteen resolutions in the last 32 minutes!" [Laughter]

And, I submit to you that resolutions passed in that speedy fashion certainly ought not to be recounted here by me and I don't know how much time you would take reading them if you had the opportunity to read them.

It might be, Walter Ruether, that we will have to reverse our attitude on filibustering and stop that kind of speedy legislation.

The urgent, recurringly stated duty upon every conferee is to multiply his experience here in the communication he will effect among his fellow citizens back home.

He must take back home this record, not only of what the Council report contains, but of the amendments, the additions, the broadening and strengthening which will become a part of the report to the President as well as specific resolutions adopted by the committees this afternoon.

Each conferee must carry the message back home, the call to community action on the local level, the stirring of interrelated and purposeful state and regional action and the wide use of the newly acquired tools and channels provided by federal policy and legislation.

The new four part civil rights bill of 1966, now at or near the committee hearing stage in both the House and the Senate, offers a chance for immediate action this summer, not next winter, on aspects of, at least, three topics of this Conference.

A section of the bill, known as H.R. 14765, broadens the authority of the Attorney General to initiate school desegregation actions without waiting for the filing of complaints by parents.

Those of you who come from affected ares know that this places the burden of enforcing United States law upon the parents who are vulnerable to the pressures that can be generated in their own community, political social and even fiscal.

So, this bill of 1966 would remove that burden from the parents and place responsibility for enforcing United States law upon the United States government.

[Applause]

Another section would close some of the loopholes in the jury selection process in both state and federal courts which now permit racial discrimination, or exclusion, in that process.

A third section is in line with our Conference's recommendation on the administration of justice in providing for the handling in federal courts of the assailants of the civil rights workers and their friends who seek the free exercise of constitutional rights.

Finally, the new legislation would ban discrimination in the sale or rental of housing, a prime target of the participants in this Conference.

Each Congressman and Senator should be impressed, in this election year, with the need for enactment of this legislation.

After every such gigantic and seemingly impersonal gathering such as this, people tend to ask "What can one person do?"

Each section of the Council report, the White Paper of this Conference, contains specific enumeration of what can be done.

But, here, in this pending legislation, now before the Congress, is a task that can be undertaken in the next twenty-four hours.

In fact, urgency is the key word not only with respect to this Conference, but with respect to the whole deadly infection of racism in our national life.

In iether intellectually patronizing or in stridently sneering tones it has been held in some quarters that conferences such as this are but "talk".

Now, the answer is that in an honest and accurate sense, they are talk, but so, too, was the Sermon on the

Mount.

So was Patrick Henry's deathless oration in the Virginia Assembly.

So were the debates of Abraham Lincoln and Stephen Douglas.

What were the lamentations of the ancient Hebrews but talk to revive their people and to restore their relationship to God and to hope?

What, indeed, were the spirituals of the slaves of our own south but talk set to the chants for a new day of freedom and dignity?

There is room always for dissent on emphasis and tactics, but none on goals.

The destiny of twenty millions of Americans and of the nation to whose welfare that destiny is bound, cannot be left solely to the doctrinaire conformists who brook no dissent and who, lately, have begun to classify believers by the color of their skins.

In this long climb, Negroes have had white allies since the first white southerner violated the law by teaching slaves to read and write.

The devils have been over-balanced, by far, by the quiet unafraid friends--the students of recent years who went into the southern hinterlands and the dedicated men and women of all three great religious faiths who have brought a new fervor and a fresh courage to the whole freedom movement.

By the friends in organized labor who were a tower of financial strength and of legislative skills in the drive for the enactment of the Civil Rights Bill of 1964.

Now, students and observers have recognized that the bravery and resourcefulness and ever-lasting energy of the Negro American have marked the climb of all our people, white and black, to an awareness of the enormous task before our country.

As the President remarked in an aside last night, the Negro has ploughed a steady furrow.

There has been this unremitting drive ahead by the black millions who, when darkness was all around and hope but a distant glimmer in the pervading night, fought their way upward.

The mood today is not one of despaire, but one of escalating expectation.

The need is for urgency because our nation's neglect of the past is about to rendezvous with a world-wide technological expansion.

The repercussions are felt from Biloxi to Bombay, to Nairobi, to London and back to Washington.

Urgency is the word.

After the Watts riot last August, the MacCone report declared and I quote:

"Our Commission has made many costly and extreme recommendations, but in addition, it called for a revolutionary attitude toward the problems of the city."

Revolutionary attitude means a discarding of the past routines, a welcome to daring, to innovation, to unorthodoxy.

It means a looking forward, not a looking back.

Undergirding all, it means a commitment to more than structure and method and even to precise objectives.

It means a commitment to a morality broader and higher than that concerned with self and group.

We must truly see others as ourselves and all as our nation, our common and glorious heritage built upon man and his freedom.

For that,is what our country is about.

If at times some of us become irritable or uneasy over the expectations of our largest minority population, let him read again the eloquent and perceptive words from President Johnson's Howard University speech.

He said:

> The Negro, like these others [thatis, the other white minorities] will have to rely mostly on his own efforts. But he just cannot do it alone. For

they did not have the heritage of centuries to overcome. They did nto have a cultural tradition which had been twisted and battered by endless years of hatred and hopelessness. Nor were they excluded because of race or color, a feeling whose dark intensity is matched by no other prejudice in our society.

And, the President concluded as we here tonight might well conclude:

He said:

For what is justice?

It is to fulfill the fair expectations of man.

American justice is a very special thing. We have pursued it faithfully to the edge of our expectations. And, we have failed to find it for the American Negro.

It is the glorious opportunity of this generation to end the one huge wrong of the American nation and, in so doing, to find America for ourselves, a home for freedom.

Thank you.

[Whereupon the entire assemblage accorded Mr. Wilkins a standing ovation.]

CHAIRMAN HEINEMAN: Will you remain standing, please for the benediction?

This will be pronounced by Rabbi Seymore Cohen

President of the Synagogue Council of America.

[Whereupon Rabbi Seymore Cohen pronounced the benediction.]

The first meeting of the White House Conference on Civil Rights, "To Fulfill These Rights" is adjourned.

[The meeting adjourned at nine-forty o'clock.]

Vol #: 2
Number: 27
Ser.: Johnson Library
Collection: WH Conference Civ. Rts.
Box: 28
File: Dinner Session 6/2

Remarks of Roy Wilkins, Executive Director of the National Association for the Advancement of Colored People, at the closing dinner meeting of the White House Conference "To Fulfill These Rights," June 2, 1966, Sheraton Park Hotel, Washington, D. C. 8:00 p.m.

This conference, which we are concluding tonight, is properly but an expansion of the revolution of rising expectations which has been in being among Negro citizens and their allies since the date of the Second Emancipation, May 17, 1954.

On that date, the legal blessing which had been bestowed for 58 years upon the doctrine of separate-but-equal constitutional citizenship was withdrawn in the historic Brown decision of the U. S. Supreme Court.

These past two days have brought the first-in-history White House Conference "To Fulfill These Rights." There have been White House Conferences on health, children, foreign policy, education and other issues vital to our national welfare. Now, for the first time, the issue which has plagued both the national policy and the American conscience from Jamestown in 1619 to Watts in 1965, has moved to the center of the national stage.

Through most of our history it has been a matter for the states and for private organizations. We have cried out our anguish, voiced our protests and worked feverishly in patchwork efforts within the States, but we lacked the national recognition of, and attention to, what we knew to be a national concern.

The handicap of the state perspective has been underscored no more effectively than by the correspondence in 1809 of Thomas Jefferson. He wrote to a friend:

"My doubts /as to the inherent abilities of Negroes/ were the result of personal observation in the limited sphere of my own state, where the opportunities for the development of their genius were not favorable and those of exercising it still less so... but whatever be their degree of talent, it is no measure of their rights."

The present civil rights struggle is essentially an effort by the Negro American minority, handicapped above other minorities by skin color and a slave background, to find, in Jefferson's words, "favorable opportunities for the "development" and "exercise" of "their genius."

Our conference today, called with uncommon courage by our President, has substituted for Jefferson's personal observation a White Paper of formidable facts, of fearless analysis and arraignment and of bold chartings of action reaching to the heart of the democratic ideal.

Since a survey of the vast variety of disabilities stemming from racial exploitation would require a month-long conference and several volumes of reports and recommendations, four critical areas of living and citizenship were selected. No mere history of hardship, this, but a frank 1966 look at the present and into the future.

On economic security and welfare: "...no more ugly and urgent crisis facing this Nation today that the economic insecurity of Negro Americans. ...employment and income problems are complex, long-standing and rooted deeply...Negro unemployment is of disaster proportions...creative and large scale action must be taken to achieve full and fair employment for the Negro working-age population."

On education: "American schools today are failing to fulfill" their purpose of preparing children "to be independent persons in an open society... It is incontestable that we have different qualities of education and therefore widely varying levels of opportunity through schooling for the Negro child and the white child...more than 90 percent (of school children) is educated in racially segregated schools.../which/ provide inferior education" through their failure "to prepare their pupils for life in our pluralistic society, and ever-shrinking world...defacto segregation continues as the prevailing pattern in the North and West, and, if anything, has become more, rather than less, rigid."

On housing: "The consequences of the slums and the ghettos and the barriers to freedom of choice in housing loom large. The dimensions of this program /of massive building and rehabilitation programs/ are staggering - but they are no larger than America's space ventures..."

On administration of justice three categories were set forth embracing protection of Negroes and civil rights workers in connection with the exercise of their rights: equal justice in the operation of the machinery of the law - juries, courts, court officials and law enforcement agents and police minority group community relations.

The material in the Council report, including the recommendations for action, has received critical scrutiny and has benefitted from broadening and strengthening corrections and amendments, including home rule for D. C., by the conferees in the twelve committees. Each of these urgent suggestions, born of intimate experience on local and state levels, has become a part of the record and will be submitted as a part of the report to the President, as will the specific resolutions adopted in the committees this afternoon.

The urgent, recurringly stated duty upon every conferee is to multiply his experience here in the communication he will effect among his fellow citizens back home. He must carry the message, the call to community action on the local level, the stirring of interrelated and purposeful state and regional action and the wide use of the newly-acquired tools and channels provided by Federal policy and legislation.

The new four-part civil rights bill of 1966, now at or near the committee hearing stage in both the House and the Senate, offers a chance for immediate action this summer, not next winter, on aspects of three topics of this Conference.

A section of the bill, H.R. 14765, broadens the authority of the Attorney General to initiate school desegregation actions without waiting for the filing of complaints by parents.

Another section would close some of the loopholes in the jury selection process in both State and Federal courts which now permit racial discrimination - or exclusion - in that process.

A third section is in line with our Conference's recommendation on the administration of justice in providing for the handling in Federal courts of the assailants of the civil rights workers and their friends who seek the free exercise of constitutional rights.

Finally, the new legislation would ban discrimination in the sale or rental of housing, a prime target of the participants in this Conference.

Each Congressman and Senator should be impressed, in this election year, with the need for enactment of this legislation. After every such gigantic and seemingly impersonal gathering such as this, people tend to ask "what can one person do?"

Each section of the Council report, the White Paper of this Conference, contains specific enumeration of what can be done. But here, in this pending legislation, now before the Congress, is a task that can be undertaken in the next twenty-four hours.

In fact, urgency is the key word not only with respect to this Conference, but with respect to the whole deadly infection of racism in our national life.

In either intellectually patronizing or in stridently sneering tones it has been held in some quarters that conferences such as this are but 'talk.' The answer is that in an honest and accurate sense, they are talk. But so, too, was the Sermon on the Mount. So was Patrick Henry's deathless oration in the Virginia Assembly. So were the Lincoln-Douglas debates.

What were the lamentations of the ancient Hebrews but talk to revive their people and to restore their relationship to God and to hope? What, indeed, were the spirituals of the slaves of our own South but talk set to the chants for a new day of freedom and dignity?

There is room always for dissent on emphases and tactics, but none on goals. The destiny of twenty millions of Americans and of the nation to whose welfare that destiny is bound, cannot be left solely to the ~~flippant~~ doctrinaire conformists who brook no dissent and who, lately, have begun to classify believers by the color of their skins.

In this long climb, Negroes have had white allies since the first white Southerner violated the law by teaching slaves to read and write. The devils have been overbalanced, by far, by the quiet unafraid friends - the students of recent years who went into the Southern hinterlands and the dedicated men and women of all three great religious faiths who have brought a new fervor and a fresh courage to the whole freedom movement. We need them and they need us.

Students and observers have recognized that the bravery and resourcefulness and everlasting energy of the Negro American have marked the climb of all our people, white and black, to an awareness of the enormous task before our country.

As the President remarked in an aside last night, the Negro has ploughed a steady furrow. There has been this unremitting drive ahead by the black millions who, when darkness was all around and hope but a distant glimmer in the pervasive night, fought their way upward.

The mood today is not one of despair, but one of escalating expectation. The need is for urgency, for our nation's neglect of the past is about to rendezvous with a worldwide technological expansion. The repercussions are felt from Biloxi to Bombay to Nairobi to London to Washington.

Urgency is the word. After the Watts riot last August, the McCone report declared: "...our Commission has made many costly and extreme recommendations." But in addition, it called for a "revolutionary attitude" toward the problems of the city.

Revolutionary attitude means a discarding of the past routines, a welcome to daring, to innovation, to unorthodoxy. It means a looking forward, not a looking back.

Undergirding all, it means a commitment to more than structure and method and even precise objectives. It means a commitment to a morality broader and higher than that concerned with self and group.

We must truly see others as ourselves and all as our nation - our common and glorious heritage built upon man and his freedom. For that is what our country is about. If at times some of us become irritable or uneasy over the expectations of our largest minority population, let him read again the eloquent and perceptive words from the President's Howard University speech. He said:

"The Negro, like these others /the white minorities/ will have to rely mostly on his own efforts. But he just cannot do it alone. For they did not have the heritage of centuries to overcome. They did not have a cultural tradition which had been twisted and battered by endless years of hatred and hopelessness. Nor were they excluded because of race and/or color -- a feeling whose dark intensity is matched by no other prejudice in our society."

And the President concluded as we here tonight might well conclude:

For what is justice?

"It is to fulfill the fair expectations of man.

"American justice is a very special thing...We have pursued it faithfully to the edge of our expectations. And we have failed to find it for the American Negro.

"It is the glorious opportunity of this generation to end the one huge wrong of the American Nation and, in so doing, to find America for ourselves...a home for freedom."

- UNITED STATES GOVERNMENT

Memorandum

TO : Harold Fleming

DATE: June 14, 1966

FROM : Evelyn Idelson

SUBJECT: Conference Resolutions

Attached are the Resolutions voted on and passed by Conference Committees. They are organized by subject area, plus addition of a "General" area. There is some attempt at category subdivision in each area, but as yet, this does not necessarily conform to the subdivisions in the Council's Report.

To meet your deadline, these have been typed very quickly, and -- for the most part -- have not been edited for grammar, style or -- in some cases -- sense.

They are submitted, therefore, as a draft only. It seems to me that a number of improvements could be made, but I thought it best to get the reaction of the high command before another retyping.

I get your points about a commitment that all Resolutions would be submitted to the President, and that certain persons have strong feelings about retaining their own language.

Where a Resolution has been thought out, written out, and involves some significant and substantive thinking, the point is well taken.

But many, many of these were being thought out on the floor, and their sloppy and diffuse wording could only embarass -- not gratify -- the authors. If the President can have his off-the-cuff remarks revised for our document, certainly the participants are entitled to the same privilege.

Without violating any promises, I still believe that these Resolutions could be edited and made much more effective. In fact, many more people might be more annoyed and feel that the content of the Resolutions could not possibly be read, valued, digested or acted upon, unless there is some consolidation and deliniation undertaken.

There are a number of Resolutions which say the same thing, where difference in wording is trivial, and where consolidation (with a note that X committees had passed such a Resolution) would make a much stronger point, and save a lot of space. I have taken the liberty of doing this for a few Resolutions which had only tiny difference of wording, but it could be done for many more.)

I also believe that it is entirely proper to break up a Resolution into different sections (Education-Housing, etc.) because the people or committees who introduced them and the Chairmen who ordered the voting made it clear in most cases that this was intended. Actually, I had separated most of the Resolutions in this way before our talk yesterday, and found it would take too much time to put them back together. I can go back and do this if you insist. I have left the Leadership Conference Resolution intact (although I think some reference to its points, i.e. housing, strengthening EEOC, administration of justice, etc. should be indicated in the appropriate subject sections.) Within the subject section, I have included a few multi-part Resolutions, but would still prefer to separate them to emphasize the particular action sought.

In several cases, a "Whereas" clause or other emotional verbiage has been included because I thought it represented the kind of personal investment which you wanted to keep, but for consistency (and with more time) I would rather work this into the actual Resolution and attempt a general style.

One important point: I believe that there were Resolutions voted on and passed in some of the sessions -- Glenda said there were some in the Housing Section -- for example. If possible, I would like those working in these sectio to forward such Resolutions for inclusion in this section.

Finally: I will be glad to put in some more time to edit and make sense out of this when you reach any further decision about format, style, etc. It would be helpful -- 'though probably impossible -- to have the people familiar with the Council's Report help put these in sections related to the Report.

Attachments:
As stated

GENERAL RESOLUTIONS

I. Conference Report Commended

1. We strongly urge the Council to adopt their report, with our resolutions, and put them into effect or seek to have them put into effect as quickly as possible.

2. We commend the substance, tone and direction of the Council's report and recommendations to the Conference, and do recommend the adoption of the same.

3. We endorse, in substance, the report of the council as a minimum start to fulfill these rights, but this endorsement would not imply that the recommendations are totally adequate to fulfill these rights.

4. The delegates expressed their appreciation to President Johnson for the opportunity afforded each of us to participate in this First Conference to Fulfil These Rights, for the opportunity to assist by recommendation and action to in fact make the promise a reality.

5. It was resolved that the members of Group III of the White House Conference "To Fulfill These Rights" commended the council on the Report and Recommendations it prepared for the Conference and endorse in broad terms the ways it has set forth for realizing the objectives essential to the achievement of a just, free, and equal society.

"In expressing this endorsement, moreover, we recognize that the Council's recommendations do not represent either a precise or inflexible prescription for action or exhaust all the means open to the nation in its continuing commitment 'To Fulfill These Rights.'"

6. The committee resolved that the Council's report in toto be adopted as a basis in principle for our discussion.

7. The committee approved the recommendations of the Council.

II. Conference Follow Up Actions Reported to Conferees.

1. Resolved that the questions and criticisms raised at this Conference be condensed and categorized and mailed to each Conference participant along with complete answers as to what the President and his administration plan to do about the eradication of the Federal Government's continued participation in practices of discrimination because of race, creed or color.

2. Urged that a further reporting of the conference be sent to all the delegates.

III. Vietnam

1. "This Committee urges President Johnson to continue and intensify his efforts to bring the war in Vietnam to an early and honorable end so that the same and even a much greater level of Federal funds and Federal leadership can be focused to fulfill these rights today."

IV. White House Civil Rights Conference For Each State.

1. There shall be held a conference "To fulfill These Rights" in each of the fifty States and the District of Columbia no later than the autumn of 1966; each shall be sponsored by the Federal Government, preferably by the U. S. Commission on Civil Rights, in cooperation with the State Government where possible; the invitees shall be widely representative of the population of the State, with particular emphasis on minority group leadership.

2. An over-all call be issued in each individual state for regional, state and city conferences "to fulfill these rights," representative of all minority groups, using the Council's findings as a flexible guideline.

   Wherever a state administration refuses to cooperate with the Federal Government in calling such a conference, the Federal Government, in cooperation with the Civil Rights and other interested groups, should proceed with the holding of such a conference and implementing their findings, even if it infringes on states rights, as a matter of national interest.

3. We should go on record, all of us, when we go home, to organize a conference similar to this in every state in order to bring more of the business community in on these conferences, and we should get the local churches within our state, especially our Southern States, to become more involved with the cutting edge of the civil rights movement.

4. This Conference requests the President to work with the governors of our States, in cooperation with religious and private groups, civil rights organizations, and State governmental organizations to invite delegates to State conferences designed for formulating specific plans to fulfill these rights at the State and local levels.

V. Recommendations for Agencies for Conference Follow - Through

1. The Conference requests the President to maintain the Council as an on-going body, and that in cooperation with the Council, he call a special conference of selected leadership groups from the private sector to respond and to report regarding what these institutions, will do to implement the conference recommendations. That such groups called into special conferences should include: religious leaders, business and labor, housing leaders, school board presidents and superintendents and governors and mayors of selected states and cities.
2. The conference requests the President to maintain the Council on a continuing basis as an on-going body which can ~~be~~ looked into and effectively act upon action of this conference.
3. The Council should be maintained as an on-going body for sometime to come; and that the President call the special conference from selected leadership groups, such as religious groups, business and labor groups, school boards, governors and mayors of selected states and cities, so that they can respond and report what they are doing with regard to the implementation of this plan after it has been presented to the American society. These people can be confronted directly with the questions of what we can do to live up to the standards of the White House Conference, To fulfill these rights. We have got to ask that this kind of action be established or we are facing a risk. History will simply draw the curtain on the this conference.

4. This body should immediately request the President of the United States to establish a broad-based Special Citizens Commission for the purpose of developing and implementing the recommendations of of this White House Conference "to fulfill these rights," and delegating to this commission a supervisory and coordinating responsibility over all federal agencies now operating in the field of civil rights, and all federal agencies dealing with any issue or practice in which the well-being of any minority group is either affirmatively or adversely affected.

5. We urge and request the President to establish the necessary enforcement agencies to take steps to ensure that the deliberations of this Conference are enforced on the national, state, and local levels.

6. The White House Conference has demonstrated the need for a permanent organization of representatives of federal, state and local civil rights agencies, private civil rights organizations, charitable and educational foundations, and interested private citizens, to meet to exchange information and discuss civil rights problems, policies and strategies.

   "Accordingly, we urge the U. S. Commission on Civil Rights to organize a permanent National Conference on Civil Rights composed of such representatives and private citizens. The Conference would meet periodically in sections devoted to particular problems and annually in general session. The Civil Rights Commission should furnish the Conference and its sections with a professional secretariat."

7. The Planning Council should remain in session for a period of one year, for the purposes of receiving from the President, and the various branches of government, a response, a direct response to the prepared recommendations.

8. This Council requests the President to appoint a post-conference White House Committee to report back to the President, the conferees, the nation, on the progress taken on each of the recommendations in the area of economic security and welfare, education, housing and the administration of justice; action taken on the suggestions for study and action taken in the area of the complaints for investigation. And that this report be issued one year from today.

9. A similar Conference should be called within one year of this date at which time evaluation will be made, and for the recomendations submitted here. Delegates to this Conference should be deputized to implement recommendations from this conference on a local level in order to "Fullfill These Rights.

10. The Council should request the President to appoint a post-Conference White House Committee to report back, one year from this date, to the President, the Conferees, and the Nation, on the progress and action taken on each of the complaints, recommendations and suggestions made here.

11. Because the proposals in the Council's Report and Recommendations will require a tremendous source of manpower to effect such proposals, we recommend that a realistic, dynamic and deliberate crash program be developed for the recruiting and training of such personnel with adequate funding.

VI. Priority, Budget and Timetable

1. The planners of this conference should be directed by the President to redraft the set of proposals in the light of the priorities, budget, timetable and federal and other governmental responsibilities. (This resolution has been adopted by four committees.)
2. The planners of this Conference should be directed by the President to prepare for this set of proposals a set of the priorities, budgets, timetables, along with the appropriate governmental responsibility needed to Fulfill These Rights.
3. The President should direct the council to prepare a budget to carry out the recommendations of this council and as supplemented by the conference.
4. This Conference recommends to the President and to the Congress that in establishing priorities for programs of action, that the entire space program should have lower priority compared to programs designed to fulfill these rights.
5. The United States should make equal opportunities for its minority citizens the number one priority. (This resolution was passed in two committees).
6. The committee feels the ruse of defense expenditures must not be used to postpone, reduce, or deny expenditures for the programs to "Fulfill These Rights". These programs are of the highest priority.

VII. Appointment of Vice President as Civil Rights and Poverty Coordinator

1. We recommend that President Johnson again delegate to the Vice President of the United States the responsibility for coordinating and expediting the federal anti-poverty and civil rights programs and that Vice President Humphrey give immediate attention to the urgent needs in Watts, Mississippi, and similar civil rights problem areas.

VIII. Home Rule

1. This Conference strongly urges the President to press for and the Congress of the United States to press at this legislative session a "Free D. C. Voting Rights Act of 1966" including provisions for an elected mayor, city council, school board, and delegate to Congress. (This resolution was adopted by five committees.)

2. This Conference "To Fulfill These Rights" goes on record urging the President to use all of his executive and his political power to secure Home Rule for the District of Columbia. (This resolution was adopted by two committees.)

3. The Conference To Fulfill These Rights supports the efforts of the citizens of Washington to obtain Home Rule now and, hence, to determine how their funds, and the Government-provided support, shall be spent to solve the existing problems of Washington, also the Conference recognizes the unique opportunity due to Federal influence to make Washington a model city and clearly show good faith in fulfilling these rights.

4. The Committee records its approval of local self government for the District of Columbia and urges the President and the Congress of the United States to grant Home Rule now to the nearly one million residents in the District of Columbia by approving this year a mayor-city council-delegate-congress bill similar to the one which passed in the Senate in July 1965.

5. We urge early enactment of legislation to return elective government to the District of Columbia.

IX. AMEND TITLE VI, 1964 Act

1. The provisions of Title VI of the Civil Rights Act of 1964 should be amended to include state, county and municipal governments.

2. This Conference goes on record expressing its outrage at the suggestion by the American Medical Association that it would be legal to discriminate against federally assisted patients by treating them in separate offices, or on separate days, or at separate hours. It is the opinion of this Conference that separate can be no more equal in health than it is in education.

   We strongly recommend to the President that legislation be presented, which would amend Title VI of the Civil Rights Act of 1964 by broadening the prohibitions to include a prohibition against discrimination on account of the economic circumstances.

X. Withhold Federal Funds Under Title VI, 1964 Act

1. We call upon the President of the United States to issue an executive order directing the Department of Health, Education, and Welfare and all other federal agencies to require strict compliance with Title VI and the regulations and guide lines issued thereunder. (This resolution was adopted in two committees.)

2. We strongly urge the President to exercise his responsibilities to guarantee an end to discrimination, by the withholding of federal funds whenever it is deemed necessary.

3. We call upon the President of the United States to give the Secretary of Health, Education and Welfare a clear mandate and specific instructions to carry out to the full extent of the law, under Title VI of the 1964 Civil Rights Act, the withholding of new Federal funds, including those of the Medicare Act beginning July 1, 1966, to all hospitals, health facilities and health departments wich are not clearly and totally found to be in compliance through the current investigative procedures of the Office of Equal Health Opportunity of the United States Public Health Service.

4. The Federal Government should take all the steps necessary to fully enforce Title VI of the Civil Rights Act of 1964, particularly as applies to health associations, and that a national conference be called immediately to deal with special health problems of Negroes and other minority groups.

5. The federal government should cease using its funds in projects which result in discriminatory practices by state and local governments.

6. The Federal Government should negotiate with common carriers, such as airlines, railroads and so forth, regarding their discriminatory practices, and in the event that substantial changes are not made forthwith, the Federal Government should invoke the provision of Title VI of the Civil Rights law of 1965 to cause federal contracts and federal subsidies to cease.
7. We recommend to the President, that a Commissioner responsible to the President be named to oversee all Federal Programs in the state of Mississippi and that it have the power to act in areas of discrimination practices by any agency using Federal Funds.
8. Federal Government should negotiate with the Seward Luggage Company of Petersburg, Virginia, regarding its alleged discriminatory practices and in the event that substantial change is not made forthwith, then the Federal Government should immediately invoke Title VI, and that Federal contracts and subsidies should cease. This is an example which should be repeated with any other company found guilty of this practice.
9. The President shall take all necessary steps to insure prompt and effective compliance with the requirements of Title VI.

XI. Restore Civil Rights Enforcement Funds

1. The Committee recommends the restoration of the necessary funds to set up adequate machinery to enforce the laws, and direct, on local level, the funds affecting Housing, Education, Law Enforcement and Economic Security.

XII. Greater Presidential Role

1. We strongly urge the President to exercise his responsibilities to guarantee an end to discrimination through use of existing measures including Title VI and Title VII and any Executive Orders which shall become necessary and which, in many instances, he has not used. (This resolution was adopted in two committees.)

2. We strongly urge the President to exercise his responsibilities to guarantee an end to discrimination.

3. This conference is on record requiring the Federal Government, from top to bottom, to enforce its own laws, and to believe in them.

4. The President use the powers of his office to the maximum extent to fulfill these rights. (This resolution was adopted in two committees).

XIII. National Public Education Program

1. The people ought to know what the civil rights are, and therefore the committee recommends that machinery be organized for the deffusion and implementation of this information. The government should bring the facts to the people by whatever means of efficacy.
2. Large amounts of funds should be provided for public relations activities so that the nation can be informed of evils of discrimination, etc., such as its loss of human resources and manpower. The committee believes that the minds, and hearts of Americans will accept changes proposed and enacted into law on civil rights matters through strong public relations programs.
4. Acts of discrimination should be viewed as criminal acts and as destructive of respectful law and order as are other criminal acts against persons and/or property. This requires an all-out effort to make use of all communications media and the resources of all voluntary organizations and opinion-molding institutions in our society.
5. The Federal Government should recognize the existence of prejudice and discrimination as a national hazard. In addition to the enforcement of laws, the Federal Government should assume the responsibility for a vigorous program of public education for the purpose of creating a national policy of equality for all in fact. It must use all of its expertise in attitudinal changes, its access to mass media, and literature in order to re-create the spirit of being a true American.

XIV. Greater Role For Women

1. It was resolved that more women should be added to the President's White House Council and that women be used on all committees pertaining to the general welfare of our group. We also feel that we should have the services and thinking of a cross section of all women on all committees of the White House where there is a need for such.

XV. Conference on National Health Recommended Now

1. It is resolved that a national conference be called immediately to deal with the special health problems of Negroes and other minority groups

Resolution on Civil Rights Law Enforcement and Passage of the Civil Rights Act of 1966

We urge that Congress strengthen the 1966 Civil Rights Bill in the following respects:

1. To provide indemity for those who suffer injury in the cause of civil rights;
2. To make the jury provisions more automatic;
3. To provide administrative enforcement for the fair housing provisions;
4. To apply the equal opportunity provisions of the 1964 law to employment by state and local government.

We call upon the Senate, in particular, to restore the $927,000 to the Department of HEW's budget; and we call upon Congress in general to assure adequate appropriations and personnel for agencies with civil rights responsibilities.

We call upon all departments of government to initiate affirmative enforcement programs, particularly with respect to withholding funds under Title VI of the 1964 Act and the assignment of voting registrars under the Voting Rights Act of 1965.

(This resolution was passed by nine committee and introduced, but not voted on, because of adjourment, in one other.)

Federal Support to Self-Help Programs

1. The Government should see as part of its responsibility the financing of self-help programs. (Such as Operation Exodus in Boston.)

Re-Evaluate Civil Service System to Ensure Civil Rights Enforcement

1. We recommend to the President that the total Civil Service system in this country be re-evaluated because a top administrator, a Secretary of a Department, and Under Secretary of a Department does not have the right to hire or fire a federal government official at the regional level who is a bottleneck and who is not carrying out the spirit and intent of the civil rights program. The Federal Government, the President and all should take a hard look at what is happening with $50 billion we are spending other than on defense.

More Participation of Poor in Federal Programs

1. It is resolved that the President emphasize the principle of maximum feasible participation of the Negro, Puerto Rican, the Mexican-American and the poor white and other minority groups in all federal programs, agencies and involvement. (This resolution was passed in five committees.)
2. This conference is on record as urging the administration and the United States Congress to fortify the rights of direct and concerted community action on the part of the victims of social injustice.

Civil Rights Commission to be Permanent Agency

1. It is resolved that the United States Commission on Civil Rights be made a permanent entity of the federal government.

Other Minorities

1. It is resolved, that the emphasis in this Conference has been to transform opportunity into achievement for Negro Americans but we also proclaim that we seek this end and goal for all disadvantaged minorities, whatever their ethnic groups or national origin, and invite them to make common cause with us "to fulfill these rights."

2. "We express our concern over setting the limits of this conference to include only Negro Americans. We stress our commitment and promise all minority citizens of this nation to pledge ourselves to strike down discrimination and prejudice against all men." (This resolution passed two committees.)

3. We urge the administration to broaden its focus and to reaffirm its concern for the problems of all our citizens.

Multipurpose Resolutions

1. It is resolved that each ~~conference~~ conferee, here because of his recognized leadership in his and her community, dedicate himself and herself to seeing that violations of civil rights laws, regulations and guidelines are promptly brought to the attention of local, State and Federal agencies charged with enforcement or compliance and to follow up for results. Each conferee should dedicate himself and herself to stirring the latent and apathetic interest of their local communities and fellow citizens in better education, in the inclusion of Negro history in the curriculum, in better school board policies, in adequate local taxes for educational purposes, and in participation in school board elections as well as those of other officials. And each conferee should dedicate himself and herself to establishing local efforts aimed at increased participation and cooperation of the people themselves, labor orgainzation and industry in achieving desirable goals in job training, job placement and ungrading of minority group workers.

It is further resolved, that the Federal Government, in its programs and legislation and guidelines should not place extra enforcement burdens on minority citizens who already have been denied rights, privileges and educational advantages; but that the burden be placed on the educational system, housing authorities and other governmental and legal structures to properly perform.

2. This Conference asks the Federal Government to expend funds for educational projects and housing programs outside of the existing formal education and housing establishments.

These funds should be made available to the Department of Education, Federal Housing Authority, OEO and other government agencies.

We strongly advise that these agencies finance the educational proposals of civil rights organizations. These organizations have effectively carried out large scale educational programs. They have prepared adults for job training, taught adult education, consumer education, and prepared youth for college. Their only limitations have been funds.

"The civil rights organizations have long standing relationships with the masses in ways that give civil rights organizations special advantages in the motivation and mobilization of the masses of the undenied.

"We resolve that the federal government should continue to try to find means of preventing State and local governments from denying Federal funds to groups that are not politically or traditionally a part of the present local political structure in power."

Broader Metropolitan Involvement

1. Because equality in employment, education, housing, and civil rights opportunities cannot be solved only for the core of various municipalities, the Federal Government shall make all efforts to involve the broader metropolitan communities in the obtaining of these equalities.

Vol #: 2
Number: 30
Ser.: Johnson Pres. Library
Collection: White House Central 14
Box: 14
File: Political Issues Raised

THE WHITE HOUSE CONFERENCE "TO FULFILL THESE RIGHTS"

1800 G Street, N. W.
Washington, D. C.
Tel: 737-9010

June 28, 1966

MEMORANDUM

To : Edward C. Sylvester, Jr.
Vice Chairman
White House Conference "To Fulfill These Rights"

From : Elizabeth W. Reeves

Subject: Political Issues Raised Outside of the Scheduled Agenda of The White House Conference

Criteria for the selection of an issue involved an appraisal of the frequency or weight of the issue, i.e. whether it was raised in two or more panels or discussed at length.

The issue itself is phrased to take in the flavor of the crux of the problem. To further define the issue, sample statements are cited by panel and page. Finally, an observation regarding the disposal of the issue is noted. The Vietnam issue being well known is hereby omitted.

NON-AGENDA ISSUES IN THE FINAL TWELVE PANEL SESSIONS OF THE WHITE HOUSE CONFERENCE ON CIVIL RIGHTS

June 1 and 2, 1966

INTRODUCTION

A sense of frustrated urgency seemed to dominate the final proceedings of the White House Conference on Civil Rights. The invitees were strongly concerned with reaching for what is attainable and practicable right now, with somehow getting to the big men who sit at the top overseeing this mass of people struggling for rights that should have been birthrights. While it was recognized that the Federal Government has done a great deal in the area of civil rights and other institutions have done too little, bewildered conferees kept reaching for a word or a way of pointing up the immediacy of needs. The Administration was repeatedly denounced for its laxity in enforcing anti-discrimination laws and prodding private industry by example.

Skepticism and disillusionment marked such foreboding or censorious statements as "...if towns like Watts go up in smoke, then we can forget fulfilling because there will be no rights to fulfill" (II, 44) or "...disaster areas in race relations cannot be righted by long, bureaucratic delays...they need immediate solution."

Aside from agenda items scheduled for the final sessions and the resolutions brought to the panels and from the floor, certain issues arose that pointed up the general mood and thinking of the participants just as the Conference was concluding. Such issues involve (1) a continuing quarrel with the conference itself, the invitations issued, and the mechanics of procedures; (2) an impatience with the "all deliberate speed" tune of the 1954 Supreme Court decision; (3) a condemnation of any emphasis on reaching the moon before settling the civil rights problem; (4) a strong aversion to saddling Negro applicants with the "qualified" prerequisite; (5) a firm refusal to cease demonstrations and marches in the battle for rights; (6) refusal to listen to the platitudes of the "good guys" - be he a respected minister or a disrespected compromiser; (7) an unyielding conviction that the President must lead the Federal Government in enforcing rights, and (8) a unified consensus that political power is the crystallization of protest and persuasion.

THE QUARREL WITH THE CONFERENCE ITSELF, THE INVITATIONS ISSUED, AND THE MECHANICS OF PROCEDURE

CONFERENCE:

Termed "exercise in interracial understanding," "talk substituting for action," a "come-on," "LSD," "waste of time," etc.

INVITATIONS:

Why not more poor people at the Conference? (X,103)...more representation of people for whom conference being conducted? (p.113)

Absence of representatives of big business at the decision and policy making level (X,147). (This charge was challenged from the floor but not resolved.)

Businessman vastly outnumbered but conference must solicit his support (VI).

MECHANICS:

CON: Participants could not offer suggestions;

Council's recommendations were to be accepted as "Holy Bible";

Debate time was limited to "squash" protest and controversial comment;

Too little time was allowed to deal in depth with breadth of issues.

Example: See pp.36-37 and p. 92, Panel I or p.49, Panel V

PRO: "Impossible to bring 2500 people together to accomplish anything had preparation not been made in advance - this number of people could not meet in two days time, get organized, and agree on anything."

OBSERVATION

It is significant that this last issue arose again during final sessions of three panels, indicating a residue of misunderstanding on part of many people as to their being limited to either accepting or rejecting Council's proposals. Nevertheless, when the Chairman or participants reiterated the fact that the Council's proposals were merely guidelines for invitees to supplement or criticize, meetings moved on.

THE IMPATIENCE WITH "ALL DELIBERATE SPEED" CONNOTATION

"All deliberate speed" is now laughable and leaves a bad taste in the mouth"; "anytime you delay justice, you deny justice"; "feasible" is a pussyfooting word. (I,66)

Deploring absence of timetables in fulfilling rights. (II,31)

Can't stomach double talk and delay like "it takes a long time," "Rome wasn't built in a day," "You can't expect miracles." (III,297)

Floor search for word to indicate no more waiting (much discussion). (IV,325)

"Deliberate speed" abhorred as a term (XII, 284); "compel," "aggressive enforcement," "now" (p.362,366); "urge" vs. "suggest" (p.380).
In answer to one participant's becoming impatient with another participant's slowness in getting to the point, the reply was that he would get there in time: "with all deliberate speed." (p. 327)

OBSERVATION

Any phrase other than "forthwith" or "now" is unsatisfactory. Some word must be used, some descriptive phrase must be employed to indicate with the greatest strength that waiting time has run out. (Six panels)

CONDEMNATION OF THE RACE TO THE MOON USURPING THE QUEST FOR CIVIL RIGHTS

Is the moon more important than the well-being of Watts? (II,31)

President should have a lower priority for space program than for civil rights. (II,72)

Don't teach child in Negro school how to shoe mules but how to fly to the moon, too. (III,297)

OBSERVATION

Above three remarks indicate varying degrees of annoyance with any emphasis on conquering space to the financial or moral detriment of conquering problems in civil rights, although as Americans, Negroes also take pride in the space conquest. (The moon versus civil rights was mentioned in five panels.)

AVERSION TO THE TERM "QUALIFIED" AS REQUISITE IN NEGRO EMPLOYMENT

CON: Argument against adding words "qualified Negro": We must assume that the government and private agencies are appointing only qualified people. Part of the stereotype regarding Negro employment is the insistence upon the term "qualified Negro." For everyone else it is simply "employment"; for the Negro, it is "qualified." (I, 62D)

PRO: Argument for using the term "qualified Negro": Dangerous doctrine to urge employment of people by race, sex, religion, or national origin without making it clear that "qualified" people must be appointed. (I, 63D)

OBSERVATION

One panel somewhat heatedly discussed whether such a conditional word as "qualified" should be used in recommending employment of Negroes to firms. Finally, a vote was taken and the "qualified" advocate lost. Two other panels struck the word without argument.

REFUSAL TO LESSEN CREATIVE TENSION THAT COMES FROM NON-VIOLENT DEMONSTRATION

PRO: "Peace is not to be desired over justice. What we seek here is justice and if we can have harmony with justice, okay; but if it is necessary to have disharmony to have justice, then justice is desired."

CON: We must reduce tensions and work towards national unity..."people who have broken the law of the land contribute to tensions that lead to violence and bloodshed...mobs and riots."

PRO: "I'm for unity and quite tired of tension...but can recommendations be passed and implemented in an era of complete tranquility...such sentiment from this Conference would be misunderstoood.

(Nine pages of discussion: VII, 294-302)

OBSERVATION

Advocates of the kind of unity to be secured through cessation of marches and demonstrations lost the floor and the vote in three panels to disgusted participants who felt that no compromise should be made that involved handing the white power structure the Negroes' best weapon.

DISMISSAL OF THE "GOOD GUYS" INFLUENCE

1. Sensitivity of Ministers to the Conference and the Conference to Them.

   "I note no one from the ministry is on that committee. It is sort of a universal rule that when they have preachers in the house that they are used for something." (I, 14)

   "We will now be particularly solicitous of the feelings of Baptist ministers." (XII, 368)

2. Concern about Placating Devices of Those Challenged

   "Image" Negroes are being appointed who represent the white power structure. (III, 278-9)

   Benefits are "handed out to the good Negroes who will stay in line and won't challenge the system." (VI, 42)

3. Tolerance of "Do Gooders" but Not Now.

   Bring out gifts of Negro into national culture...eliminate fears of failure. (X, 76-77)

   Build a better, more beautiful world where old and young will find use for themselves (VI, 29-30)

   Call on all Americans to support with sincerity and public expression the human revolution now happening in our country (IV, 455)

OBSERVATION

From Panels I through XII the voices of the ministers, of the acceptors, and of the dreamers sought hearings. The people deferred to the ministers, rejected the acceptors, and tolerated the dreamers. The mood seemed to be that Little Lord Fauntleroy has a place in the movement if he knows when to fit himself with dungarees to solve the issues at hand. (II, 44)

CONVICTION THAT THE FEDERAL GOVERNMENT LED BY THE PRESIDENT MUST ENFORCE RIGHTS

The Federal Government must take a more active role (I, 19)...the President must use his power (I, 50).

Definite need for moral commitment of the Federal Government (II, 16)... a need for immediate concern and immediate reaction (II, 44).

More persistent efforts must be made by the Federal Government to circumvent State and local statutes (III, 299).

Much of the trouble...in this country in the future, like riots, will be laid to the Federal Government which should be the law...any time the law observes a crime being permitted and does not apprehend the criminal, then the law becomes part of that crime. (V, 19) the Federal Government should carry out the law or get the law off the books.

The Federal Government must face up to defending Negroes who are defending the rights and honor of this country at home and abroad (VI, 44).

Across this country is a general loss of confidence in the Federal Government (VII, 356).

People representing the Federal Government (like Justice Department attorneys) bow to the prejudices of the white man (IX, 216).

Federal Government shouldn't have people discuss this type of stuff if they're not going to implement it. Just hush! (XI, 154)

OBSERVATION

In ten panels a dominant feeling was that the Executive Branch of the government could boldly enforce laws already passed and speedily fulfill civil rights without talk. Particularly, so-called avoidance and delaying tactics of the Department of Health, Education and Welfare and the Department of Justice were attacked.

CONSENSUS THAT POLITICAL POWER MUST REPLACE PROTEST AND PERSUASION

Need to go home and mobilize support to get affirmative action on civil rights. (I, 33)

Go back to communities to pressure by vote, etc. (II, 40)

Be aware that problem of non-fulfillment of rights can be due to apathy of people in political action. (II, 84)

Go back and work hard at city and state level to fulfill rights. (VII, 359)

Go back to our communities and put pressure on in order to get some of the things done. (VIII, 297)

Excitement of conference triggers need to work at local level to push for people and practices to fulfill rights. (IX, 186)

Return to the communities to challenge people. Use congressional elections throughout country to voice opinion on welfare, OEO, Vietnam. (X, 111,116)

Don't be afraid to challenge the demagogues in their own states (i.e., George Wallace). (XI, 153)

Votes can press for vigorous enforcement of the law. (XII, 364)

OBSERVATION

Emerging realization during final sessions that just as the Conference can help pressure legislation at the national level, so can concerted effort by local civil rights leaders change the pattern of discrimination through votes at local and national level. A great need now is to spur action at home.

NEED FOR A CONTINUING BODY TO SUPERVISE CIVIL RIGHTS STRUGGLE

Two panels suggested that the Vice President's job as liaison person to civil rights groups be reactivated. One discussant in another panel felt that too many organizations had a hand in the struggle now and one more was unnecessary.

OBSERVATION

The suggestions were not concrete and were lost for want of shape. Yet a general feeling was that this same kind of conference should be scheduled in home states.

WHITE HOUSE CONFERENCE "TO FULFILL THESE RIGHTS"

Analysis of Comments on the Role of Labor Organizations

June 29, 1966

Approximately 55 speakers mentioned the role of labor organizations in the provision of equal employment opportunities for Negroes. About 45 of these conferees made unfavorable references. Only 4 speakers expressed the view that discrimination by labor unions was not a problem--all 4 of these individuals represented labor organizations at the Conference.

The Conference participants who expressed the view that many labor organizations engaged in discriminatory practices came from a wide range of backgrounds and affiliations. They included representatives of civil rights organizations, churches, Federal Government agencies, local and State governments, educational institutions, and business enterprises. Of special significance is the fact that representatives of several unions accepted the prevailing view concerning the extent of discrimination among labor unions. For example, a UAW representative said, "Now, obviously I am not here to criticize the labor movement. I am a part of it. But I do not believe there are 25,000 Negroes in the whole building trades and that could very well spill over into some industrial unions...."

In general, the remarks implied that union discrimination was predominantly a local problem, rather than resulting from action by national or international unions. Although most speakers did not identify specific geographic areas where discrimination is practiced, a few areas were cited. Among them were St. Louis, New York City, Chicago, Syracuse, Detroit, Cleveland, and New Orleans. Other speakers mentioned entire States, e.g., North Carolina, Iowa, Delaware, Maryland, and Virginia. It is obvious from the statements of the conferees that discriminatory patterns in both the North and South require attention.

By far the greatest concentration of allegations of discrimination concerned the craft unions, particularly in the building trades. Specific references were made to discrimination among brick layers, plumbers, electrical workers, glaziers, pipefitters, ironfitters, and sheetmetal workers. For example, one speaker said, "Now, in our State these unions practice total exclusion of Negroes. We have no Negro bricklayers, no Negro plumbers, no Negro sheetmetal workers, no Negro ironfitters--you can go right down the list."

A St. Louis NAACP representative said, "All of you have read about the Gateway Arch in St. Louis, and it is an abomination to anti-segregationists, because after millions of dollars had been spent in erecting that Arch, it finally came down to the level of a sub-sub-sub contract on which an integrated union could make a bid, where a few token Negroes could get employment, and then the big AFL-CIO claimed a jurisdictional dispute...."

One speaker from a Southern city did mention that Negroes are admitted to local unions of carpenters, cement finishers, brick layers, and plasterers, but this speaker bitterly stressed the discriminatory practices of all other unions in his area. Aside from building trades unions, allegations of discrimination were made for local unions of railroad workers and of machinists in the South.

A number of conferees made recommendations for eliminating discrimination by unions. These included:

1. The formation of new non-discriminatory unions in areas where existing unions discriminate.

2. Stricter enforcement of Federal, State, and local equal employment opportunity laws.

3. Action by the AFL-CIO to enforce anti-discrimination policies among its member national and local unions. For instance, a speaker from Minneapolis said, "What I don't understand is why there has to be so many levels of policy-making and why there cannot be at the national AFL-CIO headquarters a policy that would cover all states. Just as we have suggested that the Federal Government in its legislative acts makes.... policies that are uniform throughout the Government, why can't we do this with unions?"

4. Federal assistance for Negro building contractors and other businessmen as a means of opening up new job opportunities for Negroes in the skilled trades.

Because of the importance of apprenticeship as an avenue for entering the skilled trades, substantial attention was given by the conferees to this method of training. There was a definite and recurring sentiment that many labor organizations engaged in discriminatory practices in apprenticeship programs.

Of 16 conferees who discussed this point, only 4—all union representatives—indicated the view that no substantial discrimination exists in apprenticeship programs. The remaining speakers complained about the lack of equal opportunities in this field. A Southern educator remarked, "I think that we must recognize that one of the great barriers to increased participation on the part of Negroes in the labor market is the refusal on the part of labor unions that masquerade as liberals to let Negroes into their apprenticeship programs. If you can't get into the apprenticeship programs, you never get to be a bricklayer or electrician."

Replying to the argument that Negro youths cannot meet the standards for admission to apprenticeship programs, a UAW representative said, "Where you talk about qualified Negroes, the building trades and industry know what the standards are long before the youngster leaves high school.... they know....the training programs there in high schools....whether this youngster is going to be able to pass an apprenticeship examination before he gets his diploma. So who is kidding who?"

Another union speaker said, "It would appear to me here, if we are going to make any .....any progress here, at least this Committee or this Conference should do something new on the matter of apprenticeship, because if we keep the apprenticeship training program as we have it now, it will take us 200 years to get rid of all discrimination."

Specific recommendations made by conferees to eliminate discrimination from apprenticeship programs included:

1. Expansion of pre-apprenticeship training opportunities to help Negro youth qualify for apprenticeship programs.

2. Expansion of the number of apprentices.

3. Review of apprenticeship programs to eliminate unnecessary content and to shorten the training time.

4. Tax incentives to encourage an expansion of union training programs.

5. Stricter enforcement of Federal, State, and local equal employment opportunity laws.

6. Information programs to interest Negroes in the skilled trades and ensure their access to apprenticeship programs.

7. One speaker recommended the abolition of formal apprenticeship programs and the substitution of new training approaches.